DIARY OF A SAILOR

S.S.R WAYTE

INDIA • SINGAPORE • MALAYSIA

ISBN
Paperback 979-8-89673-822-0
Hardcase 979-8-89744-989-7

CONTENTS

Acknowledgements 4

Introduction 5

PART 1: SAILING EUROPE SECTOR 7

1. ITALY 9
SALERNO 10
LIVORNO (Leghorn) 12
LUCCA 13

2. SAN MARINO 19

3. GENOA 22
Genoa Lanterna 23
Joining Ship at Genoa 23
Palazzo Reale 25

4. MARSEILLES, FRANCE 29
Hangout Place in Marseille! 32
The Repair Berth 34

5. SÈTE, FRANCE 44
Biscuits from Sète 46
Musée Paul Valéry 48
Cimetière Marin 48
Mont Saint - Clair 49
Les Pierres Blanches 49
La Marine 49
Le Vieux Sète 49

6. VALENCIA, SPAIN 50

7. LISBON, PORTUGAL 55
Cristo Rei Monument 58

PART 2: SAILING AFRICAN SECTOR 59

8. SENEGAL 61
REPUBLIC OF SENEGAL 61
Dakar (14°40'N; 17°26'W) 62

9. REPUBLIC OF IVORY COAST 64
Flora and Fauna 65

10. ABIDJAN (5°19'N; 4°01'W) 66
The Third Engineer's Strange Allergy 66
The Jamaican Stowaway 69

11. COTONOU, BENIN 6°21'N; 002°26'E 75
History 75

12. LUANDA, ANGOLA 78
History 79
Health 79
Flora 80
Fauna 80
National Game Reserves 80
Chief Produces 81

13. LIBREVILLE, REPUBLIC OF GABON 82

14. DOUALA, UNITED REPUBLIC OF CAMEROUN (4°03'N; 9°41'E) . . .85
Joining Kwanza 85
Flora 88
Fauna 88

15. THE SEAMENS CLUB 95
THE CON ARTIST: Part 1 - The Lady 97
THE CON ARTIST: Part 2 - The Friend . . . 98

16. SAN PEDRO 102
Meme* the Pilot 104

17. POINTE-NOIRE - THE PEOPLES REPUBLIC OF THE CONGO 108

ACKNOWLEDGEMENTS

Most of the writings and photographs are my work. I have quoted from other papers whose sources are unknown to me. All such quotes are duly acknowledged. Other copyright infringements, if any, are purely out of ignorance on my part. My apologies and due acknowledgement of the same.

INTRODUCTION

There was a time, not very long ago, when men captured the power of the wind in sails to cross the oceans on wooden ships. Since they were predominantly working with sails, they were called sailors. Technology has come a long way since those days, and man no longer depends on the wind and sails to power his ships. Yet, men who work on the ships continue to be called sailors.

So, yes, I was a sailor. I worked for different companies that operated different kinds of ships on various routes. So I did get to visit many parts of the world.

People often want to know how much of the world I have seen. There is a difference. Tourists invariably end up in regular tourist destinations with particular objectives. The sailor, on the other hand, goes where his ship takes him. As long as there is enough water for the ship to safely navigate.

For a few years, I worked for a Shipping Company that traded between Europe and West Africa. Through this book, I take you with me on these trips so you can see a small part of the world through the eyes of a sailor.

The crew on a ship is divided into 3 departments, each with its own functions. The Navigating Department looks after the Navigation, of course! The team of navigators on board is responsible for taking the ship safely to its destination by plotting a suitable course and then steering the ship accordingly. The Navigating Department also takes care of the loading and unloading operations. Remember, the ship is floating on water. So movement of weights will affect the balance of the ship. Navigating officers are also trained in Marine Law and related matters so that they can someday take charge of the ship as Captains. In all legal matters, the ship is treated as a person and the Captain is the voice of the ship.

Then you have the Engineering Department. The engine room of a ship today bristles with machinery. A big engine, called the main engine, turns the propeller which will push or propel the ship through the water. Generator Engines produce enough electricity to meet the ship's requirements. Freshwater Generators convert seawater to freshwater. HVAC (heating, ventilation, air conditioning) systems to make the air on board safe and comfortable to live in. Refrigeration Plants preserve food for the voyages. Ancillary machinery such as pumps, blowers, and oil purifiers.

Then there is machinery on deck such as cranes to handle cargo, winches to open and close the hatches and to raise and lower the anchors. Yeah, mind-boggling!

Last but not least, the Saloon department, which feeds us all. The cooks prepare the food and the stewards attend to housekeeping and keep the accommodation clean.

Until a few years ago, we also had a radio officer on board who would communicate with the rest of the world using Morse Code. Rapid developments in modern technology have now given us satellite telephones on board the ship.

I have taken a few liberties! I have not taken permission from any of the people who play a part in my adventures mentioned here, so their names are not disclosed.

I have also not followed any standard template for all places visited because this is not a reference book. It is meant to be a laid-back, cool trip on a ship!

Statistics given, such as population, are mentioned only so you have an idea of the relative size of the place. Population is a variable depending on when the census was taken. Please do take all data with a pinch of salt!

Part 1

SAILING EUROPE SECTOR

The purpose of a cargo ship is to earn freight, so it needs to be constantly in operation. Most of the crew is comfortably settled on board, but when it is time for them to leave the ship after completing their tenure, the new crew has to chase behind the ship to catch up and get on board. We shall do that later. Let me first familiarise you with the route we usually take. We are on a ship already completing its operations and sailing out of Valencia, Spain.

From Valencia, we went to Livorno, Italy, and here we had visitors from the head office in Switzerland. They came to see the ship since it was a new acquisition.

The next day, some friends picked me up from the ship, and we drove to a town called Lucca, about 60 kilometres away from Livorno. This was a bonus visit.

From Livorno, our next stop was in Genoa, Italy, but it was a Sunday, so no one disturbed us. We finished cargo work and sailed out peacefully to Marseilles, France.

Marseilles is our refuelling halt. The ship burns something like 65,000 litres of fuel a day, and we have to take on 210,000 litres. The job requires extreme concentration because we take oil pollution seriously, and a small accident can bring down heavy retribution. After 6 hours, we were all quite tired as it was past midnight when we finished the refuelling operation. The next day, I had some free time and took one of the engine cadets for a company and went ashore. We found ourselves in an area called Arab Street, and I bought some almonds and raisins. You get good pistachios as well, but it was enough for this time. Next, we went perfume shopping. My wife's favourite is Oscar de la Renta, but I was not able to find a shop that had stock. Instead, I bought J'adore, Anais Anais, and Flower (Kenzo).

We then had an Arabic-style Big Mac at an Egyptian shop. A huge chunk of mutton is suspended and slowly being turned and roasted. The man shaves off slices of the meat, which he puts inside a king-sized bun along with slices of tomato, onion, and a white sauce. It is called a Doner Kebab, and it tastes good.

I have seen this in the Middle Eastern countries where it is called Shawarma.

Finally, it was time to take the bus back to the ship.

Marseille is a city of many cultures. You have Egyptians, Algerians, Tunisians, Vietnamese, Africans, and Indians. A visit to Marseille is like travelling to many parts of the world simultaneously. All cultures have small restaurants around the old port (Vieux Port) area, and at night, it is a gastronomic delight.

Back on the ship, we find all work in the port has stopped. On another ship, they had been unloading a boat, and one of the workers had been standing in the boat to let go of the ropes after the boat touched the water. The rope broke, and both the man and the boat fell into the water. The port closed for 12 hours as they did not want any movement while they searched for the body. They never found him.

Our last stop in Europe was Valencia again. It had nice, pleasant weather and warm sunshine, but we arrived in the evening and sailed in the morning. Besides, it was a long walk to the gate in Valencia, so no one was interested in going ashore.

As you can imagine, it was a busy fortnight, and we enjoyed a small break out at sea as we sailed to West Africa.

ITALY

For the most part, Italy consists of a peninsula, extending 805 kilometres from the Alps and varying from 113 to 240 kilometres in breadth. The coast is sandy, and much of the country south of Naples is of volcanic origin. The principal rivers are Fiume Arno, Cecina, Ombrone, Tevere, Garigliano, and Volturno. The highest peak, 3000 metres high, is 96 kilometres northeast of Rome and is covered with snow for 8 months of the year.

After the fall of the Roman Empire, the country consisted of a number of small, independent states. The Kingdom of Italy came into being under the House of Savoy in 1870 after a struggle lasting 20 years. The final stages in the unification of the country were the ceding of Lombardia by Austria in 1859 and Venezia in 1866, and the evacuation of Rome by the French in 1870. In 1871, the King of Italy entered Rome, which was declared to be the capital.

During World War I, Italy fought against Germany and at the Peace Treaty, received some former Austrian territory, including Trieste. Benito Mussolini was the leader of the Fascist Party from 1922 to 1943. Italy entered World War II on the side of the Germans but after being invaded by the Allies in 1943, it signed an armistice and thereafter supported the Allies. The fascist regime was abolished and during the hostilities against Germany, Mussolini was executed by resistance fighters.

The party was abolished after World War II.

In 1944, King Victor Emmanuel III retired in favour of his son, Prince Umberto, although retaining the title of King of Italy until his abdication in 1946. Shortly afterwards, a national referendum was held, and the majority favoured a republic. The Royal Family then left the country. At the Peace Treaty in 1947, Italy lost most of the territory gained in World War I but retained Trieste.

Agriculture forms an important part of the national economy with the chief crops being rice, wheat, maize, grapes, and olives. Tobacco is a government monopoly. Fishing and tourism contribute significantly to the economy. The main railway system is state-owned and covers more than 16,000 kilometres, half of which is electrified while 285,000 kilometres of roads and 5000 kilometres of motorway traverse the country. Al Italia, the Italian Airline, operates worldwide. In the mid-70s, the Italian Merchant fleet was the 9th largest in the world. Italy has an area of 301,268 square kilometres and a population of 60 million. Italian, a Romance language derived from Latin, is used throughout, but there are many dialects showing French, Spanish, German, and Arabic influences.

SALERNO

Impressive Entrance to Salerno

To the Left: Salerno Port

Five kilometres NNE of Capo d'Orso rises Monte San Liberatore (465m) and, from the southeast, presents a distinctive profile.

On the eastern side is a white building and a conspicuous cross which is illuminated from 1900 hrs to 2300 hrs in summer and 1700 hrs to 2100 hrs in winter. A prominent castle in ruins stands on the crest of a hill 2 kilometres east of San Liberatone and overlooks Salerno.

Carmine Nuovo, 5.5 cables east-southeast of the castle, has a square belfry surmounted by a cross. Salerno has a population of about 135,000.

Bridge at Salerno with Mount Arechi

Castello Arechi

The Cathedral of San Matteo, Salerno

I have come to this pretty city so often, and I have always eyed an old castle on top of a hill called Castelo Arechi. I never got around to visiting it, so this time, I was determined to go. When I asked the agent, Giovanni, how to get up there, he said it would take about an hour of heavy trekking.

"But there is nothing to see there except the castle ruins," he said.

"Not worth it," he added.

"What, no guide, no tour, no one to explain the castle?" I asked.

"Nothing! The only thing people go up there for is a panoramic view of Salerno," said Giovanni.

"What else is there to see in Salerno?" I ask.

"Have you seen the Cathedral of San Matteo?"

And that is how I got to see the Cathedral of Saint Matthew where, allegedly, his bones rest.

In the first century, Saint Matthew's body was taken from Ethiopia to Brittany (France) and from there to Velia. They did not remain in Velia for long as from the north came Alarico's Visigoths, who were looking for Africa. Later from the south came the Saracens by sea. The escaping Velians took the body with them and buried it at Lucania, and there it was forgotten. The body was recovered in the 10th century and transported to Cappaccio, a town about 30 kilometres south of Salerno.

In 954 AD, Gisulfo I, Longobard, Prince of Salerno, decreed that the relics be shifted to the capital of the Princedom, Salerno, where they remained.

On 13th December 1076, Roberto II Guiscardo defeated the last of the Longobard princes and captured the city, thus beginning the Norman Empire in South Italy. In order to win over the good wishes of the local people, he decided to build the cathedral in honour of Saint Matthew.

Built in a record 4 years, the cathedral occupies 5810 square yards in the centre of the old part of Salerno. As we enter, we find ourselves in a huge courtyard with a corridor running on all sides. The king believed that all matters conducted in the vicinity of the church would be honest. Since there was no conventional town square in Salerno, this ultimately became a sort of meeting place for the local inhabitants. Along the sides of the corridor, some tombs and marble plaques commemorate the sons of Salerno.

The church door is a huge, bronze door with 27 panels for each shutter, each with little figurines of Jesus Christ, the Virgin Mary, and Saint Matthew. The door was made in Constantinople in 1099. Inside, the ceiling of the church seems to be miles above us! The 3 apses signify the Holy Trinity. The one on the left has a mosaic of the divine Hand symbolising the voice of the Father, the central apse celebrates the Deum Natum, and the right one has a figure of the Holy Dove, remembering the Holy Ghost.

We descend a few flights of steps into the crypt. The crypt of a medieval church was used as a place in which Saints were buried. Saint Matthew's grave is in the middle of the room. A seated bronze of Saint Matthew (17th Century) captures the attention. Paintings and frescoes adorn the ceiling, and mosaic patterns (coloured marble inlay work) on the walls and the pillars are awe-inspiring. Interestingly, this was not built together at one time but contributed to by people at different periods. So we have predominantly Roman and Baroque styles and a total collection of art. The people of Salerno are lucky to have such a wonderful monument in their presence and consider Saint Matthew to be their Patron Saint.

LIVORNO (Leghorn)

Livorno is situated on a wide plain backed by hills. Livorno was an industrial city. The chief industries are shipbuilding, ship repairs, and oil refining. The city has a population of about 160,000.

Docking is an important aspect of a ship's life, during which time it is taken out of the water for inspection and maintenance work. Our company decided to drydock the ship at Livorno. We entered a huge dry dock. As there was enough space left, another ship was docked behind us.

We finished our docking on schedule, but the other ship had a serious problem with the propeller shaft, and we ended up trapped in the dock for about 40 days!

Some of us visited the city of Pisa and even ventured on a two-day visit to Rome, but short visits did not interest me. Other places of interest in the vicinity attracted us when we had a long stay in Livorno.

LIVORNO CITY

A *strange tale*

Mr. Giovanni was our agent in Livorno.

When he was a young man, he had very rugged skin on his face with many bumps and lumps. This made shaving very difficult as he always had cuts and bleeding. One day, he was sitting with his fiancée when a wasp buzzed around them. So he swatted it with a newspaper, and it fell somewhere. They searched but could not find it.

A little later, Giovanni felt the wasp crawling up under his trousers where it stung him. He squashed it to death, of course. Strangely, from the next day onwards, his skin started to clear up! The rugged skin became smooth, and his shaving problem was solved. What was that? What fate made the wasp insist on stinging him even though it cost the wasp its life?

LUCCA

Archaeological finds and documents all point to the existence of Lucca during Roman times.

In 89 BC, Lucca became a *municipium* and by 56 BC, it was important enough for people like Caesar, Pompey, and Crassus to meet here. Lucca is one of the few towns in Italy with its defensive wall system still intact today. The first defence circle was built during the Roman times, and very little of it survives today in the Church of Santa Maria Della Rosa.

In 570 AD, Lucca became the centre of the Longobard administration and the capital of Tuscia Province. The oldest religious buildings in Lucca date back to this time. Silk working became the main activity of the community, and powerful and rich businessmen with trading centres throughout Europe dominated the society. In the 1500s, Lucca became an independent republic.

To protect its liberty, a wall was built around Lucca. Construction of the new wall was commenced in 1554 and completed only in 1650. The wall is 12 metres high. Internally, at the base, it is 30 metres thick. On the bastions, barracks—buildings that housed the guards or acted as storage for ammunition—can still be seen. In the mid-19th century, the walls were planned and planted with trees to make a public walk. The total length of the walk is 4 kilometres.

The republic came to an end when the French occupied it in 1799. From 1805 to 1813, Lucca was the principality of Felice and Elisa Baciocchi. Elisa was Napoleon Bonaparte's sister, and under her, the city prospered. When Napoleon fell, the Baciocchis were driven out, and the administration of Lucca was passed on to a Duke.

The birthplace of the famous composer Giacomo Puccini, Lucca, is about 60 kilometres by road from Livorno. I was fortunate enough to visit this quaint town along with some friends from Germany which included a couple, their daughter, and their niece.

We parked outside the city walls and walked along Viale Giosue Carducci. The brick wall (fortification) runs all around the city, and we entered through a gate called Porta San Pietro (gate of Saint Peter). Most of the roads are cobblestoned, and there is hardly any traffic. A few minibuses run, and you can hire bicycles to pedal your way around. An ideal town for tourists to visit, with old monuments, souvenir shops, and restaurants. The weather was perfect, and we enjoyed our stroll.

There are signs pointing to a Tourist Information Office, and we follow them to Piazza Napoleone—an open square with an imposing statue in the centre, surrounded by nice trees and benches.

Plan of Lucca.

Piazza Napoleone

After getting all the information we needed, we walked down Via Brocheria until we came to Piazza San Michele. Here stands a grand church built with limestone on an earlier Roman structure. A wedding was going on inside the church, so we could not go around, but it is an impressive structure with a statue of Saint Michael dominating the facade.

We cut across Via Buia to Via Fillungo, the main street in town. Following the signs, we arrived at the Piazza Anfiteatro (amphitheatre), which gives us the impression of standing in an ancient colosseum.

Dating from the 2nd century AD, this was originally built outside the city by the Romans. When the original amphitheatre fell into ruin, it was used as a quarry, and all the stones were removed to construct other buildings.

At the same time, private houses were built around the original elliptical structure of the theatre. In the mid-19th century, the area was again redesigned for public use, and visitors can still enjoy it today.

In the amphitheatre, I chatted with a girl who was running an interesting antique shop. A sextant for £1500, a painting for £3000! I just did not have any change in my pocket or else I would have bought a few things, I jest. Such money is too much for me.

A short distance away is Piazza San Frediano, and the church there has an impressive mosaic facade.

Piazza San Frediano

Piazza dell' Anfiteatro

The girl at the information office told us that the best pizzas in town were at a restaurant called La Felice on Via Buia, so we retraced our steps to a really small pizzeria with those stand-up-and-eat arrangements. A Quattro Stagioni and a chilled mango juice went down nicely. There were a few more important places to see, but we had covered most of the nice places, and we were running short of time. So back to the car, back to Livorno, and back to the ship!

Highlights of Lucca

Palazzo Mansi

An aristocratic building of the 16th century is now converted into the most important museum in Lucca. It contains an imposing suite of rooms on the main floor with frescoes and salons with tapestries. The picture gallery includes valuable paintings.

Church of San Paolino and San Donato

The only monumental-sized religious building still standing inside the walls of Lucca.

Church of San Michele in Foro

This was built in white limestone on the site of an 8th-century building. The square occupies the space of an ancient Roman Forum.

Via Fillungo

The busiest street in town, where all the shops and restaurants are situated

Church of San Frediano

Known to have existed since the 12th century, the church has been regularly modified.

While I was away, there was action on the ship. The stowaways had complained that the food they were being given was not tasty, so the immigration authorities had sent some police to investigate. The second officer, a young lad of 22 years, being on duty, escorted the police to see the stowaways. The stowaway produced 2 packets of hashish (marijuana), and when the police asked where he got it from, he pointed to the second officer. The police immediately turned tough. They snatched away the walkie-talkie from the second officer and would not let him speak to anyone on the ship. They started to browbeat him with questions, and the poor boy became a nervous wreck. Meanwhile, the drugs were taken ashore and when tested, were found to be more than 2 years old. Our company had bought this ship about 2 years ago and renamed it. The police, after checking the records, were satisfied and so left the ship, but it was an unpleasant experience, especially for the second officer.

SAN MARINO

During the 4th century, a stonecutter called Marino came to work on the construction of the harbour at Rimini. The Romans were persecuting the Christians at this time, and Marino, unable to bear the torture, fled to the mountains. Some other believers followed him, and they lived in a commune. A Roman patriarch (a noble lady) who converted to Christianity presented all the land they were occupying to Marino.

After the Roman Empire fell, there was much struggle and fighting. Marino's successors built 3 castles on the Titan Mountains (750 metres) for which the place became famous.

The Titan Mountains

My friends picked me up from the ship at 1545 hrs, and we drove 70 kilometres south from Ravenna along the coast to our destination. San Marino is the smallest independent republic in the world. It has an area of 60 square kilometres and a population of 33,660.

If an outsider marries a local girl, he is not given citizenship. If a local man marries an outsider, the girl is entitled to citizenship. In no case are the children of such couples given citizenship.

We drive through the city of San Marino and then up a steep road to the first castle on the Titan Mountains. We park at the base of the castle and enter through a stone gate.

Narrow, winding paths...

City Centre

Narrow, winding, steep paths lead us upwards. On both sides are shops catering to the tourist trade. This place shuts down when it snows in winter. So the tourist trade is very important, and the people are polite and courteous. Apart from the shops, there are many restaurants and museums. We visit the Snakes and Reptiles Museum. There are many others—Ancient Arms, Wax Works, Torture Instruments. I am curious, but we do not have the time as this is a day visit.

The city centre has the Government House where there is a Statue of Liberty. The panoramic view is splendid, and it was a clear day, we were able to see the Adriatic Sea.

I bought some coins, a few stamps, and a guidebook. My friend bought some cherries, and in between, we had an ice cream. One needs a million dollars to enjoy shopping here. I was reluctant to leave this beautiful place, but it was dinner time.

About 50 kilometres before Ravenna is Gatteo a Mare, one of the many beach resorts on the Lido Adriatico. The place is a square block of buildings with rooms on the first and second floors and restaurants and shops on the ground floor. The rooms appear to be timeshare units. The central square has an open seating area, a church, restaurants, and so on. We had a beer and pizza, a stroll around, and did some window shopping. There is a

Lots of shopping

horse-driven carriage, and one can hire tandem cycles to have a good time. And thereby ended a wonderful day.

The Adriatic Coast

GENOA

Genoa, a municipality with a population of around one million, extends along the coast between Punta di Crevari (44°25'N; 8°44'E) and the east end of Nervi, 21 kilometres east-southeast. In addition to Genoa Centro, the actual city, there are several coastal towns which are grouped together as Grande Genoa. All these towns show an unbroken line of buildings along the coast and extend to the slopes of a steep range of hills at the base of Appennino Ligure. Genoa Centro can be easily recognised as its buildings extend farthest inland. The city is built like an amphitheatre on the slopes of the hills.

Grand Old Lady in Genoa Port

Porto di Genova is the Principal Port of Italy. While approaching, a number of forts, some of which are conspicuous, are visible:

1.	Forte Sperone	Massive Fort with a light-coloured roof
2.	Forte Begarto	Red Roof
3.	Forte Castellaccio	Massive, a reddish tower with 2 radio masts
4.	Forte Ratti	Long, a low building with a round tower
5.	Firte Richelieu	a grey square surmounted

Genoa Lanterna

The Genoa Lighthouse is situated northwest of the east entrance. It sits on a square tower on a building that is 76 metres in height. A signal station consisting of a black and white chequered house surrounded by a metal framework mast stands at the base of the light structure.

Joining Ship at Genoa

I left home on 12th July at 0730 hrs and was travelling to Bombay by the 0900 hrs Jet Airways flight. All went according to schedule, and on arriving, I took a taxi straight to the office at Churchgate.

La Lanterna

After completing formalities at the office, I moved to Hotel Windsor (Fort area) and after checking in, went to the doctor for a medical check-up. I then gave my measurements to the tailors for boiler suits and returned to the office (boiler suits are supplied by the company).

At the close of the office, I had dinner at the City Kitchen before returning to my room at the Hotel Windsor. City Kitchen was a favourite of mine during my training days in Bombay. Run by an ex-seafarer, they served authentic homestyle Goan food at reasonable rates.

I went to the office the next morning. Around lunchtime, I went to the Great Eastern Shipping office at Crawford Market to meet a batchmate of mine who worked there. We had lunch at a nearby restaurant, and we promised to get together again for dinner. Plans changed, and in the evening, we drove across town to another batchmate's place. After a few drinks, we ordered some rich takeaway food (Chicken tandoori, etc.) and had a pleasant evening together. By 2100 hrs, I was getting anxious about the time, and I had to practically plead with my friend to drop me back. He drove like a madman, and we made it back to the hotel in record time.

My Air France flight from Bombay to Paris was scheduled to depart at 0140 hrs on the 14th. I had the aisle seat, and at the window was a young religious fanatic type of fellow, so we did not converse much. I spent the time watching the movies—Collateral Damage and Count of Monte Cristo—and napping.

I arrived in Paris at 0730 hrs local time. My next flight to Genoa was at 1115 hrs. So, I had a mini breakfast, changed the currency to euros, and browsed the shops but did not buy anything.

The aircraft was a small one, and this time I had the window. Next to me was a Filipino seaman, and the time passed pleasantly. It was a great view of the approach as we flew low, past the lighthouse and the berth where we usually dock. The airport is a little beyond the harbour, so it was a wonderful flypast.

Genoa Old Port foreground. New Port in the background

There is the Genoa Aquarium in the old harbour area, which the family and I visited during their trip.

The agent met me at the airport. The ship had not yet arrived, so I was taken to a hotel in the heart of the city.

Genoa: Plan of the old port

Hotel Aquila & Reale is an old building. There is an old-type cage lift, and the rooms have wooden floors and old-style furniture. Modern amenities like a geyser and air conditioning have been put in, and it was comfortable. The TV was not connected yet. No fancy stuff like bellboys and so on. Just 2 ladies and a gent at reception, chambermaids, and restaurant staff.

I had a wash, and an hour later was out for a stroll. The hotel has a great location. Directly opposite the main train station called Stazione Centrale and a bus terminus of the same name. In front of the hotel stands an imposing statue of Vittorio Emanuele II, Founder of Genoese.

Most shops were closed, as it was a Sunday. Only a few Tabacchi and the shops in the railway station were open. I walked down via Balbi up to Piazza della Nunziata and within a few minutes, came across the Museo di Palazzo Reale.

Palazzo Reale

Located opposite the Chiesa (church) S Carolo, the Palazzo Reale was actually the residence of nobility added to and sumptuously decorated by 2 great Genoese families—the Balbi, who built between 1643 and 1650, and the Durazzo, who enlarged it at the turn of the 18th century, as did members of the House of Savoy some 100 years later.

The palace is the largest 17th and 18th-century building in Genoa to preserve all the fixed decorations (fresco and plasterwork) as well as the movable furnishings, paintings, and sculptures.

The ceilings have frescoes by leading artists, and the paintings exhibited include works by the foremost 17th-century Genoese artists. The palace has a rich collection of ancient and modern sculptures. The wealth and variety of its art collections drew artists and travellers to the palace throughout the 18th century. Napoleon declared it of great interest, and in 1824, King Charles Felix of Savoy chose it as the Royal Court in Genoa.

I was up early on the 15th morning and expected the agent to pick me up around 1000 hrs after the office opened. So I decided to blindly catch a bus across to another terminal. Route 33 goes from *Stazzione Principale* to *Stazzione Brignole*. The conductor told me it was a 20-minute ride, so I took a return ticket, costing me 0.77 euros. The ticket was valid for 90 minutes from the time of punching in and can be used for buses and trains.

From the station, the bus climbed steeply along the side of a hill, and we soon had a panoramic view of the harbour below. These beautiful buses were built by BREDA. (When I was in school/college, the suburban electric trains in Madras were built by Breda.)

Genoa is one of the oldest cities in Italy. Its main roads still have cobblestones. Many of the houses are made of stone with wooden shuttered windows, all in the old style. Thick bushy trees line the sides of many of the roads. I pass Stazione Nicola, Corsa Paganini, Magenta, Museo Archeologico, and arrive at Piazza Raffaello de Ferrari (via XX Settembre). Then through Via Luigi Cardona Coarte, Via Cassimorti, and Pieno Le Fondome before arriving at Stazione Brignole.

I got off the bus and crossed over to the station entrance where I loitered around for a while. I then noticed a big park and a slope (hillside) with a lot of colourful flowers, arranged like an English Coat of Arms.

The park is called *Piazza Verdi*. This is the place from where the city bus tours and the long-distance buses start.

The colourful flowers on the slope of the hill are named after Queen Victoria. It was time to head back, so I caught the return bus. The bus passed Teatro della Corte and drove along Via XX Settembre, at the head of which is Piazza Ferrari. Via Settembre is the main road of Genoa.

The average July temperature is 27 degrees. The city has a cultural, artistic and historic past and is worth exploring. Genoa was selected as the cultural capital of Europe in 2004. There are many splendid palaces, churches, museums, and galleries to see. The maze of narrow alleys (the famous *caruggi*) in the old town, particularly in the Sottoripa area, is really worth walking through to get a feel of everyday life in Genoa. There are many food shops, bars and cafés crammed into these alleys. Green pesto is a tasty Ligurian seasoning for pasta, and its wonderful smell hangs in the air.

Genoa old Harbour

Life expectancy in Genoa is one of the highest in Europe.

Ravioli is a traditional snack made from chickpea flour and mixed-fried fish (farinata). It goes well with excellent local wine or beer.

Slipping into the routine, I did some exercise this morning. At 0630 hrs, steward Akram brought coffee and told me about the stowaway. I was not even aware there was a stowaway on board, but apparently, we had one.

He was isolated in a cabin on the Main Deck, and this morning, around 0200 hrs, he broke the bars of the cabin and jumped from the Main Deck onto the pier, which was about 30 feet below the Main Deck. He injured himself, and the police and ambulance had to be called in. Apparently, he suffered broken ribs and was bleeding from the mouth, but there was no report of internal damage.

At 0200 hrs, Deck Seaman Swain heard some noise and stepped out into the alleyway. Suddenly, the stowaway's cabin door opened, and the stowaway stepped out into the alleyway. Swain woke up the African driver next door, and they went out on the deck to search for him. They could not spot him, but when they looked over the side, they saw him lying on the concrete pier in a pool of blood. Did he jump? Did he fall by accident?

Later the same day.

Cargo was almost finished, and we were preparing to sail at 1330 hrs. Cadet Praven was driving a forklift down the ramp from 4 to 3, lost control, and the forklift toppled over. It was a bad accident, and he was very, very lucky. A few stitches to the head and a fractured small toe on the right foot.

MARSEILLES, FRANCE

Marseille is the principal seaport of France and it extends 6 and a half kilometres along the coast. Cap Janet, a steep yellowish point, rises to a plateau that overlooks the northern part of Marseille and on which stands a large seminary. The port has 3 principal sections consisting of the Nouveau Port in the north, Porte de la Joliette, and Porte Vieux, the old natural harbour to the south.

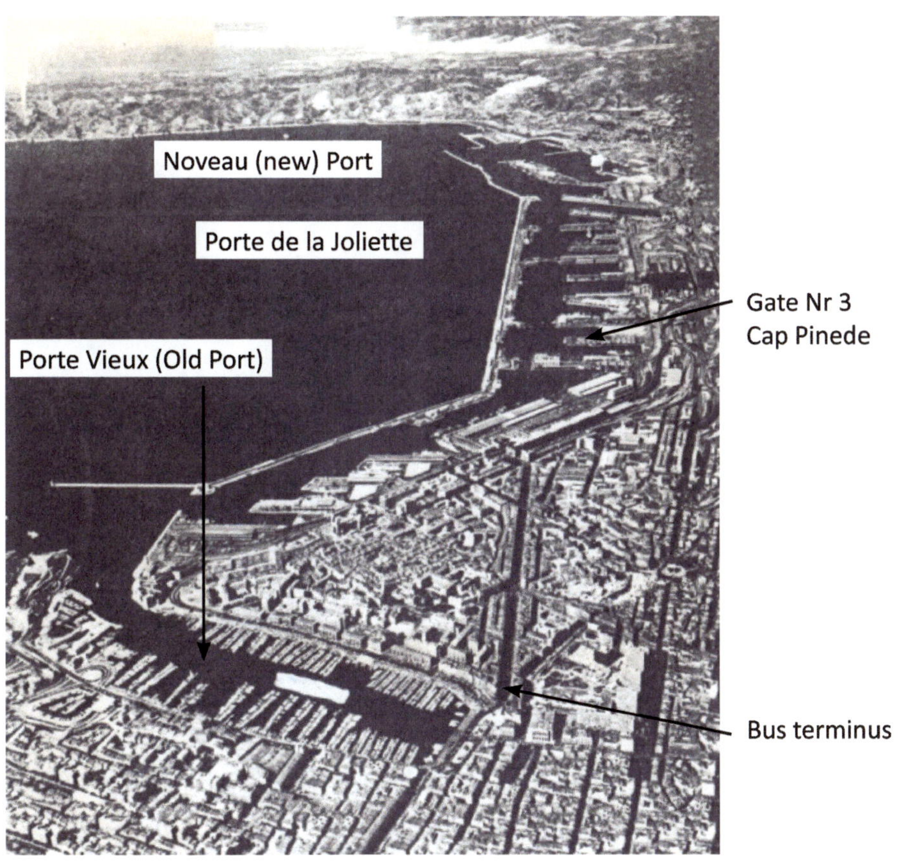

Port of Marseilles

Wall paintings indicate the region was settled more than 28,000 years ago. Surrounded by a ring of hills including the impressive Calanques, the city today winds 70 kilometres along the Mediterranean and has a population of one million. The sunshine and the mistral winds gave it that special light which inspired many famous painters.

Extensive damage was suffered during World War II (1939-1945). Marseilles has since been rebuilt and development work continues. The town is situated on the slopes of the hills that surround the old port. One mile SSE (south-southeast) is the Church of Notre-Dame de la Garde, situated on the summit of a hill 162 metres high and has a gilded statue of the Virgin Mary over its belfry.

Greek (originally called Phoenician) sailors landed at the old port in 600 BC and founded the original city of Massalia. They set up trading posts, and the city expanded with trading and fishing being the main occupations. In 49 BC, Massalia took sides with Pompeii against Caesar, who promptly laid siege to the city for 6 months, reducing it to famine before the Roman Empire conquered it.

The Romans called the place *Marsillia*. The hill served as barracks for a unit of Roman soldiers who did guard duty, watching over the city. Later, the cathedral was built, and that is how it came to be called *Notre-Dame de la Garde*—our Lady who guards.

The city later played an important part during the Crusades.

Marseille has had its ups and downs, but the most painful experience was the plague in 1720 AD, when close to 50,000 people died.

In 1792, six hundred people marched to Paris to join the French Revolution singing *The Hymn of the Army of the Rhine* (composed by a local man), which became known as *La Marseillaise* and is now the National Anthem of France.

On 22nd August, we berth at the Nouveau Port which has 5 basins. Ours is *Bassin de la Pinède* and we usually tied up at *31 Quai de la Pinède*. The gate remains closed on Sundays, but if you flash your passport, the gate is opened for you from a remote location! Fascinating!

We would be using gate no 3, and at the gate (Cap Pinède), Bus number 35 arrived promptly every 20 minutes. We bought a single journey ticket costing 9.0 Francs, and we could travel any distance for one hour. It was a 10-minute ride to the old port.

From there, we walked up a nice broad road called the Canebière and at a main intersection, turned left into Arab Street.

Canebière

Marseille is a truly multinational city. It has Arabs from Tunisia, Algeria, and Morocco; Africans from West Africa, Indians from Pondicherry, and Chinese from Vietnam (Indo-China). Each has brought along with them their own cuisine (restaurants) and culture (shops).

The area we were in was definitely Arabic, but there was a strange blend of French as well. Arab gowns and skull caps were visible on the men, but most ladies were dressed in modern fashion. The electrical officer and the third engineer are with me. We walked along Arab Street for another 5 to 10 minutes before coming to a shop called SPIGOL where we bought almonds, raisins, pistachios, and walnuts by the kilo. We had an early dinner (1730 hrs) at McDonald's just across the road and then spoke to home from the phone booth, using Taj Mahal phone cards. A 50 Franc card gave me about 18 minutes of talk time. Bien!

We then walked all the way back to the bus stop at the old port.

It was a pleasant walk as there was much to see. Many shops to window shop from, fine impressive buildings, and restaurants. There was a *Continente* department store, but we walked away from it. There was a *Nouvelle Galleria* near the bus terminus. I once visited a super shopping area called *Barne Oud*. One would need 2 or 3 days to shop here.

Hangout Place in Marseille!

In May, my wife and 2 sons sailed with me on the ship, and we visited the Basilica Notre-Dame. The captain and his family were also with us. We called for a taxi from the ship, and a Benz car arrived. The second son was excitedly jumping around on the seat, saying, "Hey, Benz da! Benz da!" Each of us has different interests! The taxi fare worked out to 100 Francs. We found our way around and took a city bus for the trip back from Notre-Dame to the old port.

Train from the old port to Notre-Dame.

I saw later that there was also a sort of toy train that ran during the tourist season, down to the Vieux Port Bus stop.

Back again at Marseilles, this time on a Sunday. Shops in town will be closed, but the Ship Chandler told us about Le Pis—a weekly open-air Arab market for all spices and nuts just across the road from the main gate.

Electrical officer, Fourth Engineer and I leg it over to the Aux Puces (pronounced Peace) flea market after breakfast.

Le Pis is a market selling the usual fruit, vegetables, and provisions, and with a few other sundry shops like restaurants, shops selling old television sets, and so on.

The actual market is housed in a big hall, and you can buy food products here from Wednesday to Sunday, antiques from Friday to Sunday, and second-hand goods on Saturdays. On Sundays, the huge parking area is converted into a flea market selling clothes, shoes, sunglasses, inexpensive watches, paintings, pots and pans, and plants.

In another corner, there was all second-hand junk, used parts for home appliances, and so on. These people are mostly Moroccan or Egyptian, so the market is popularly referred to as the Arab market, although they do not like being called that. They belong to France and liked being called French.

I was not interested in buying. Just wanted to see what it's all about and observe the people. After spending some time browsing the flea market, we strolled into the hall where the food products were, and I ended up buying 2 kgs of almonds and 2 kgs of raisins. This will help me when I am dieting, I thought. We then went to an Egyptian restaurant and ate Doner Kebab. Slices of meat are put vertically on a skewer and slowly roasted. The meat is finely sliced off and put between bread with lettuce, tomato, fried potato, and a thick layer of cholesterol—a creamy white Tartar sauce. Tastes sinfully good!

Monuments of interest in Marseille:

Abbaye de Saint Victor
The abbey was built in the 5th century by Jean Cassien on the burial place of Saint Victor, a Roman martyr who died in the 3rd century.

Arc de Triomphe
The Porte d'Aix stands at the entrance of the city; built in 1825, the triumphal arch was erected by Penchaud to the glory of the republic. The world-famous Arc de Triomphe is in Paris.

Corniche J.F. Kennedy
It is the coastal road that links the city centre to the outlying villages. The viaducts going over the valleys date back to the second century.

Cathédrale de la Nouvelle Major
This is an imposing 19th-century building in the Romanesque-Byzantine style.

Chateau D'If
This is an old fortress that Francois built in 1524. It became the state prison in the 17th century.

Marseille has many museums, beaches, and markets. The most popular ones are fish markets, markets for fruits and vegetables, flowers, and flea markets for second-hand goods.

The Repair Berth

After discharging cargo, we were shifted to a repair berth that was on the breakwater. I mentioned earlier that the port has 5 basins. All of them were protected from the sea by a long seawall (called a breakwater) running parallel to the coast for about 4 kilometres. We were also 4 kilometres away from the gate. I can comfortably walk 3 kilometres so whenever I say 4 kilometres, it only means very far away and that I cannot count more than 4.

The ship was the *Kwanza* and we were being rescheduled for the Europe-Africa trade. That meant we would have to wait for our turn in the line to come up. We needed to have a steady loading and discharging of cargo at all ports so the ships could arrive and depart at regular intervals, following a schedule.

Repair Berth, Basilica Notre-Dame in the background

Notre-Dame de la Garde from Vieux Port

The wall is 7 metres high and on top of it is a path, about a metre wide with one-foot thick walls, ideal to go for a run in the mornings or for a leisurely stroll after dinner. We did see some of the locals jogging here but it was more popular with the amateur fishermen who came to try their luck. I usually walked for about an hour on the wall each morning but one fine day I decided to hop onto a bus and go into town.

At a cafe near Vieux Port, I sat for a cup of coffee and watched Marseille come to life. The fish stalls on Quai de Belges were being set up, machines were sweeping and washing down the roads, and young people were distributing newspapers (free editions). Looking down on us was the Basilica Notre-Dame, catching the first rays of the sun. As I finished, the schoolchildren started to arrive, and people were buying their cigarettes and getting ready for another day.

A marble slab on the pavement at Vieux Port commemorates the exact place where Greek (originally called Phoenician) sailors landed at the old port in 600 BC and founded the original city of Massalia.

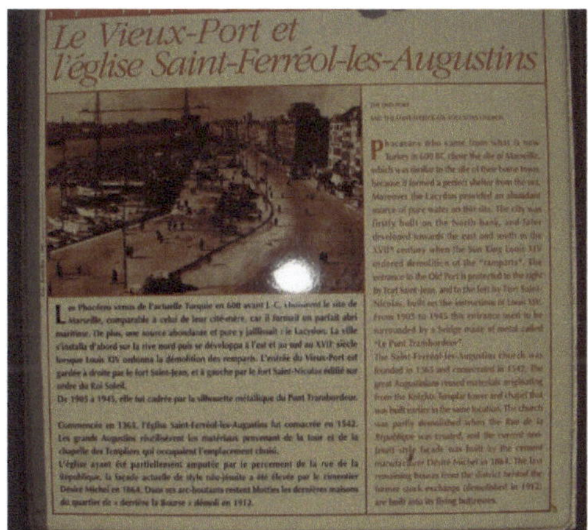

First Landing 600 BC

A Bus Tour of Marseilles

It was Sunday. We had a clear, blue sky with warm sunshine, and the temperature was 32°C—an ideal day for *Le Grand Tour* of Marseille in an open-top, double-decker bus.

The round trip would take 1.5 hours and there were 16 stops. We could hop off whenever we wanted and join the next bus. It was convenient because the buses start every hour from the old port, the first one being at 1000 hrs. The ticket was 16.00€ and was valid for one day.

We arrived early to make sure we did not miss the first bus and walked around the famous Quai des Belges Fish Market. The market is open every day of the week from 0800 hrs to 1300 hrs. I could identify some fish, and some I could not. Price markers were put, and it was interesting to see what was the most expensive fish. I was amazed to see a small-sized bream selling for €30.00 (Rs. 1560.00) a kilo! The same fish, called Sankara in Tamil, sells for 1/20th the price in Chennai.

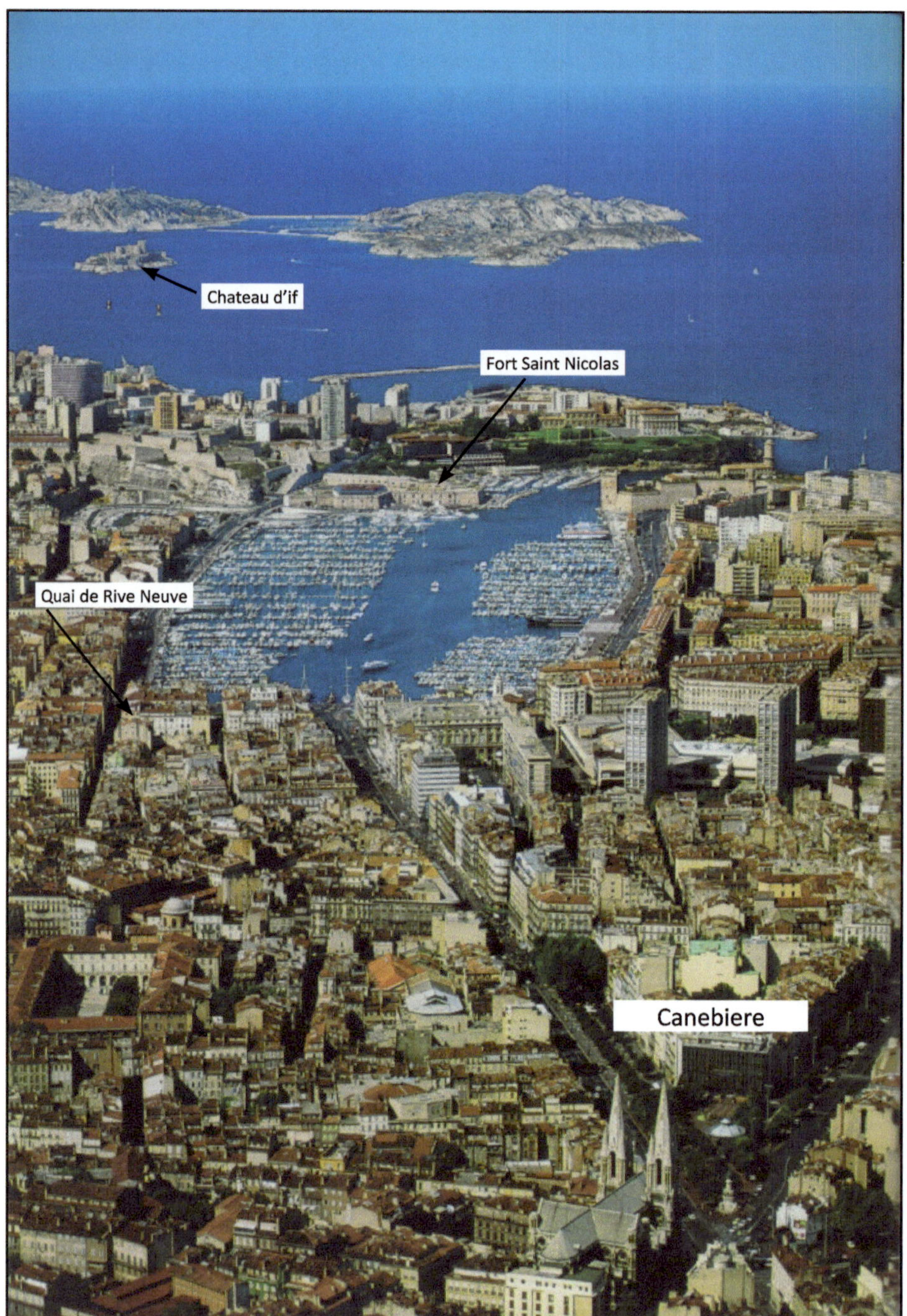

Bird's-eye view of the old port

There was a big crowd of people waiting to take the train trip to Notre-Dame de la Garde, but there were just a few of us for the bus tour—a family of 3, another couple, and us.

The driver came around handing headphones which were ours to keep. Once plugged in, you could choose to have your commentary in French, English, Italian, German, or Spanish. We drove down one length of Vieux Port along Quai de Rive Neuve and passed the star-shaped Fort Saint Nicolas built in 1680 by the Chevalier de Clerville under the orders of Louis XIV.

Fort Saint Nicolas: Entrance to the Old Port

Monument to the Dead

A little beyond, to our right was the Palais du Pharo. A big building with a nice garden, it was a gift to Napoleon III from the people of Marseilles, but the royal couple never stayed there. Now we were driving along the coast and passed Vallon des Auffes, a tiny fishing port that had a very picturesque setting, and we could see many seafood restaurants. We passed an arched gateway—the Monument to the Dead of the Oriental Wars.

Across the water, 20 minutes by boat, is the island fortress of Chateau d'If, made famous by Alexandre Dumas in his classic novel, *The Count of Monte Cristo.*

After driving for about 10 minutes along Corniche President John Kennedy, we left the coast and drove up a steep road. We were passing through the Rougas Blanc area where

Approaching the Basilica

the rich merchants of the olden days used to live. A lot of trade used to take place with Egypt. Some of the old houses were still standing, and it was easy to imagine what a great life the rich merchants would have had.

Basilica Notre-Dame de la Garde.

We were climbing to the highest point of the city where stands the Basilica Notre-Dame de la Garde.

The first chapel was built in the year 1214. Later, in 1524, a fort was built, and the present Basilica, which is in Romanesque-Byzantine style, was consecrated in 1864. It was dominated by a gold-covered (gilded) statue of Mary that could be seen from all over the city.

The esplanade around the Basilica offered the most splendid views of the city.

After the visit, as we drove down the hill, we passed a small garden named after P. Puget, a great artist from Marseilles. We then passed the Abbaye de Saint Victor, built in the 5th century over the burial place of a Roman martyr of that name who died in the 3rd century. The tour guide advised us to get off here and taste a local speciality called Navettes. These were orange or Ainese flavoured cookies and reasonably nice. We rejoined the tour route at the coastal road again, a little after Jardin du Pharo.

Driving further along Promenade Georges Pompidou, we came to Parc Balnéaire du Prado, which was the popular beach of Marseille. It was not an impressively big beach, but it was divided into sections, each having gravel, sand, and shingle.

The coastline of Marseille is mostly rocky in nature and is more famous for its Calanques or rock formations. Some of these white rock formations rise to 300 metres.

Almost at right angles to the beach was the Avenue du Prado—a narrow, straight, tree-lined road which we would be driving down. At the junction where the road met the beach was the statue of David (a replica of Michelangelo's famous David) made from Carrara marble by Cantini in 1903. Carrara is on the west coast of Italy and is famous for its white marble.

Calanques of Marseille

To our right, we passed Parc Borély, where the Annual International Boules championships are held. Boules is a game played with palm-sized steel balls that you roll along the grass. The French call it *Pétanque*, and Marseille is the international centre of this game.

At the first roundabout, we made a slight detour to visit the Stade Vélodrome. This temple of Marseille football fans was built in 1937 and after a subsequent renovation could now hold 60,000 people. It is elliptical in shape because it was first used as a cycle racing track. Marseille is very proud of its football team. The famous player Zidane is from Marseille and their team Marseille Olympic were European champions in 1993.

At the roundabout, our road took a left turn, but it was still called the Avenue du Prado. The locals referred to this road as the Champs Elysees of Marseille.

We came to the Place Castellone where stands a big column with an intricate base featuring many figures and a fountain. We have a photo.

Castellane on Avenue du Prado

Intricate fountain base

An extension of it leads to the Place Jules Guesdes where there is the Arc de Triomphe (also called Porte d'Aix), built in 1825 as the entrance to Marseille. Parallel to us and on our left was the Rue Paradis where all the Consulate buildings and the international business offices were located.

We then passed through the shopping district of Prefecture where you could shop for Haute Couture and French chocolates. The place even smells expensive.

At the Place de la Préfecture, we took a left turn and passed the Palais de Justice, an impressive building both in terms of architecture and sculpture. A right turn and we were back at the Vieux Port.

We drove on the opposite side and passed the Fort Saint Jean built in the 15th century by the Commander of the Hospitallers of Saint John of Jerusalem. King Louis XIV had a watchtower built by the Chevalier de Clerville around 1670.

Our last stop was the Cathédrale de la Nouvelle Major.

Cathédrale de la Nouvelle Major

This is the main Cathedral of Marseille, but it is not as famous as Notre-Dame de la Garde. We hopped off the bus here to admire this 19th-century building whose interiors were made in marble and porphyry. It was lunchtime now, so we decided to grab a *Doner Kebab*. There were quite a few restaurants on the Canebière that sold Egyptian food.

Very close to the Vieux Port and on the Canebière was the Marine Museum, which was in the Palais de la Bourse or the Stock Exchange building. The museum itself consisted of 2 parallel corridors, each about 150 metres in length, with engravings, paintings, and some excellent ship models that captured the history of the port since the 16th century.

Marine Museum

Marine Museum

Public Transport in Marseille

Bus Ticket

Bus Tour route

Palais Longchamp

Many Passenger Ferries call at Marseille

Palais Longchamp is the Municipal water tower built at the same time as the Marseille Canal in 1839. The complex, which includes the Museum of Fine Arts and Natural History, was completed in 1869.

A side road off the main Canebière

Side road off the main Canebière

Museum of Fine Arts

SÈTE, FRANCE

ocated between the Mediterranean and the Thau Lagoon (Etang de Thau) in France, I have to say the Fishing Port of Sète is one of the prettiest towns I have ever visited. The fishing trawlers moor in the canals that crisscross the heart of the town and reflect the colourful facades bordering them. An aerial view gives the impression of an island connected to the mainland by floating ribbons of sand.

Built on the order of King Louis XIV, the Sun King, Sète has linked the Mediterranean to the whole of the Languedoc region via the Canal du Midi for more than 3 centuries. Blessed with blue skies and sunshine for 300 days a year, Sète is called the Blue Island.

Mussels and Oysters were farmed in the Lagoon, which in some places reached the depths of 30 metres and was surrounded by hills. From early springtime, Sea Bream spawn here before returning to the sea at the first signs of the Autumn Mistral.

The canals of Sète were the scene of a legendary sport called *joutes nautiques* (jousting on boats). Sitting next to a *sétois* (inhabitant of Sète) on the stands set up along the quayside of the Canal Royal for the Feast of Saint Louis was the only way to experience this spectacular combat. The water sport is called Joutes (jousting), and the winners are given memorable nicknames.

On the blue boat and the red boat, 2 men watch each other. Each balanced on his *tintaine* (a gangplank in the stern, projecting over the water), his lance raised in a salute to the imaginary Gods. The White Knights stared at each other with contempt and in total silence. The sound of fife and drums broke the silence and sounded the attack. The lances are lowered and aimed at the opponent's *pavois* (shield). The shock was brutal! One of the figures slipped, lost his footing and fell into the canal. This ceremonial battle goes back centuries and returns to Sète on Saint Louis' Day on the 25th of August each year. True heirs to the knights of the Middle Ages, the jousters choose their king every year. The most famous was Louis Aubenque called The Terror, who won the tournament 9 years running. As no one could match him, he attacked the wooden bridge over the Grand Canal and, with his lance, stopped the boat dead, pitting his strength against more than a dozen oarsmen. That was in 1749, and the people of Sète still talk about it.

The main attractions for tourists are the sky, the sunshine, and an offshore sandbar beach, 12 kilometres long.

The region is famed far and wide for its fish, shellfish, and lobster. It is not enough to have tasted *Bouzigues oysters* and the inimitable *Tielle* without trying Sète's delicious pasta dish known as *Macaronade* and its mussels and squid stuffed with herby mincemeat. These are all delicious, but so are the *Rouille de Seiche* and *Bourride* eaten on the quayside during the *Fête de la Gastronomie* in June each year, after a glass of Muscat or with a regional wine. Some of the specialities:

Biscuits from Sète

Biscuits have traditionally played a great part in Sète's life. The *Navette Cettoise* is crunchier and bigger than the traditional biscuit. The Macaroon is a small round biscuit made with white of an egg and sugar, with the addition of powdered almond. The Madeleine, shaped like a rounded shell, comes in multiple flavours—orange blossom, lemon, or dipped in chocolate.

Les zézettes de Sète

This is a long, uniquely shaped crunchy biscuit covered in sugar crystals, made with local rose wine that gives it a wonderfully delicate flavour. Les zézettes go well with Muscat, Champagne, and ice cream or simply with tea and coffee.

Frescati

Otherwise known as *Gateau Sétois*, it is over a century old and is of Italian origin. The sweet pastry base contains raisin biscuits generously soaked in rum. This is then topped with soft Italian meringue and coated with layers of fondant coffee cream.

Le Pastissou de Sète

This biscuit combines aniseed essence with thin slices of green olives.

Bourride de Baudroie Tielle
(Stuffed mussels and baby squid)

Tielle

This is a pie containing octopus, tomatoes, and spices. It was once used as a meal for fishermen going out to sea. This unique dish, with its round shape, unusual edging, and lovely orange colour, is found *only in Sete*, where it was invented. It can be eaten hot or cold, preferably with a glass of local dry white wine.

Muscat Wine

Herault County produces many wines, but the most famous is the Muscatel. These straw-coloured, naturally sweet wines are made from a single grape variety—the small grape from Muscat.

Muscat Grapes

Their vinification includes chemical sterilisation of the Grape must by adding eau-de-vie during fermentation. They are thus rich in alcohol and sugar. The land in this region is ideal for these wines with their flavour of raisins and honey. (Note: Grape must is the freshly pressed juice of grapes, which contains the skins, seeds, and stems. It is the first step in the winemaking process. The word 'must' comes from the Latin phrase vinum mustum, which means young wine.)

There are 4 different AOCs: Frontignan, Mireval (the most famous), Mediterranean Mist, and Lunel. A new addition to the AOC is Saint-Jean-de-Minervois.

Our ship makes regular visits to Sète.

We had another full day in this favourite place of mine. It was a bright sunny day. We walked around in the morning and then sat in a cafe to send picture postcards to my friends.

I walked into a restaurant and treated myself to a plate of Tielle. It is considered a speciality of this area (Sétoise). On the

La Marine

waterfront, the Tabacchi girl recommended *Chez Francois* or *La Calanque* for lunch. The first place was too crowded, so we went to La Calanque. We had *Rouille de Seiche*, half a dinner plate of big chunks of Oyster (calamari) in a Tartar sauce, side helpings of boiled carrot, cucumber, steamed rice, and bread, of course. *Rouille de Seiche* is another speciality of this place. The other dishes I need to try in Sète are *Macaronade* and *Bourride*.

The next morning, at 0630 hrs, I put on my walking gear and walked all the way to the top of Mount Saint Clair. It took me just half an hour one way, so my morning walk was very pleasant indeed.

On top of the mountain was a sort of monastery/hotel named *Auberge des Jeunesse*.

The lights are magical at night!

Regions surrounding Sète show activity from Roman times in the 2nd century. To engage the tourist, the small town has developed a few places of interest:

Musée Paul Valéry

On display at the museum were archaeological collections, the history of the jousts (jousting on boats), pictorial works, and a room devoted to the poet Paul Valéry.

Cimetière Marin

This cemetery is immortalised by Paul Valéry in his poem *Le Cimetière Marin*.

Centre Régional d'Art Contemporain (Exhibition for Regional contemporary Art)

The point of this exhibition is to show visitors the various creations of local or internationally renowned artists.

Mont Saint - Clair

The top of this hill, which rises 183 metres above sea level, offers a panoramic view. It has a chapel dedicated to the Virgin Mary of La Salette built in 1861 on the ruins of a hermitage.

Les Pierres Blanches

For the inhabitants of Sète, one of the favourite places to stroll around is the viewing table, offering a splendid and unrestricted view over the sand bar.

La Marine

Walk along the Canal Royal to the fishing port and the Criée (electronic auction fish market) near the Marina.

Le Vieux Sète

Discover an old district of Sète, the Quartier Haut. Its architecture and buildings are closely linked to the history of the town.

VALENCIA, SPAIN

We arrived at Valencia on a bright, sunny day, and as soon as we started Cargo Work, we spotted 2 stowaways trying to run away from the ship. We managed to catch both of them but as we were taking them up to be locked in cabins, one of them broke away and tried to escape. Max, the dog, chased him and brought him down. Turned out that one of them had been hiding in the provision store all along. So he was helping himself with all the milk, fruit juice, fresh fruit, vegetables, eggs, ice cream, and the works. After putting them into individual cabins, we kept Max outside to guard. Around midnight, we heard Max barking and people rushed to see why. One of the fellows had broken the porthole glass, grabbed a lifebuoy and jumped into the water. When we spotted him, we found him swimming *towards the ship!* After jumping in, he found the water was too cold and now he wanted us to save him. When we picked him up, the poor fellow was shivering from the cold. Now Max was the hero of the ship, and he sat in sunglasses, basking in the sunshine, sipping his cool drink while the poor Chief Engineer had to work all day.

The next day, 17th August, was a Sunday. Some years back when my wife and sons sailed with me, they were in Valencia on a Sunday, and we went to Redondo—a flea market. So, I decided to go again, for old times' sake.

Custom House inside the Harbour

Bus stop outside the gate

I took bus number 4 from outside the gate. There used to be a gate, but it was all removed, and people could freely walk in and out. The bus fare was 0.90 Euro, and the final terminus was in the city centre at *Plaza de la Ajuntamiento*.

Plaza del Ajuntamiento

Fountain in the Plaza

Small quiet streets

In the centre of the Plaza was a big lawn with flower beds containing many pretty flowers. A big fountain dominated and the hiss of water was so loud that it drowned the sounds of traffic around us. To one side was an old-style Spanish building, the City Hall, which also housed the Municipal History Museum. Directly across was another magnificent old building, the main post office.

We were in the city centre, but there were many small quiet streets. One such street was the extension of *Calle de San Vicente*. A one-hundred-metre walk brought us to the *Plaza de la Reina*. We walked along the side of the cathedral and the *Miguelete Tower* to the *Plaza Virgen*.

It was a beautiful day. The weather was pleasant with a gentle breeze, and the sky was clear and blue. There was no rush of traffic or people on the street. As you can imagine, the walk was just great.

Miguelete Tower

Plaza de la Reina

The Plaza de la Reina is another green zone, but the Plaza Virgen is a hardtop with a fountain and a reclining figure. Cultural events were held there.

Last time, this complete area was occupied by a flea market run by Spanish Gypsies, but there was no sign of them this time. In a corner of the Plaza de la Reina stood a tall tower—the Church and Bell Tower of Saint Catherine. Almost at the foot of the tower was a Tourist Information kiosk. I got some brochures, and when I inquired whereabouts of the flea market, I was directed to Plaza Redondo. It was a circular, open courtyard and there were shops, but mostly being run by people of African origin. There were African wood carvings, wristwatches, and Music CDs. One shop sold pet birds, and on a side street, people were selling small puppy dogs. They were really cute, and I would like to take one home, but I knew it was impossible.

I got back to the ship for a late lunch. The Spanish word for beach is *Playa*, and Valencia has a really nice beach called *Malvarrosa*. I had been there with the Captain earlier. I have heard that it is known for nightlife during the summer months.

Plaza Virgen

Valencia also has a fine aquarium. We grabbed the opportunity to visit once. In those days, we thought the dolphin show was excellent!

Dolphin show (1) Dolphin show (2)

Dolphin show (3)

A Part of the Aquarium

Peseta Obverse Peseta Reverse

The unit of currency in Spain is the Peseta.

LISBON, PORTUGAL

The Portuguese are attracting tourists now by trying to sell it as a shopping centre. There are 4 main areas.

A) Some of the more traditional shopping streets of Lisbon are in the town centre and Chiado. The town centre streets are geometric in design and between Rossio and Terreiro do Paço, they have hundreds of shops. Chiado has many coffee shops and bookstores.

B) The Avenida da Liberdade runs from Restauradores to Parque Eduardo VII and serves as an extension of the town centre. This area has many international-branded shops.

C) Campo de Ourique has nicely laid out buildings and attractive streets, giving it a different atmosphere.

D) A calm area with large pavements makes The Roma Guerra Junqueiro and João XII Avenue a favourite shopping area for the locals. Even if you don't shop, a pleasant walk along these avenues is worth it.

But Lisbon is not all about shopping. There is much to see and do. There are many ancient and modern monuments to be seen, cuisines to be enjoyed, and cultures to be explored.

I first visited Lisbon in 1995 when I was working on a ship called LADY M. We were at the cereal berth on the other side of the river, just before the bridge.

Bridge across the Tagus River   **Aquarium Entrance Ticket**

From Belém Pilots, we had to steam for about 1½ hours up the Tagus River and pass under the Ponte 25 de Abril (Bridge) before arriving at the Container

Terminal. On this particular call, we decided to visit the aquarium, which locals claim is the biggest in Europe. Capt K.C, Electrical Officer Radha*, 3/E James*, radio officer Kumar*, Cadet Unni* and I (6 persons) pile into 2 taxis to visit the *Oceanario de Lisboa.*

The local currency is the Escudo and 200 of them make a dollar. The fare for each taxi came to 1200 Escudos, so it was a good distance further up the river. In 1998, Lisbon hosted the EUROPA Expo 1998, for which they specially built this commercial centre. The Oceanario (Aquarium) is just one part of the complex. One would need a week to really go through it, and we had only a few hours.

The aquarium was nice. Built around a huge central tank, it housed the big sharks. Split into 2 levels, the building itself was impressive, not to mention the well-maintained and interesting exhibits. Man's ingenuity had excelled itself.

The tourist season was just picking up with some of the early ones already starting to arrive, but there were many schoolchildren as well. There were concessions, but the normal entrance fee was 1,700 Escudos, which works out to Rs. 370.00.

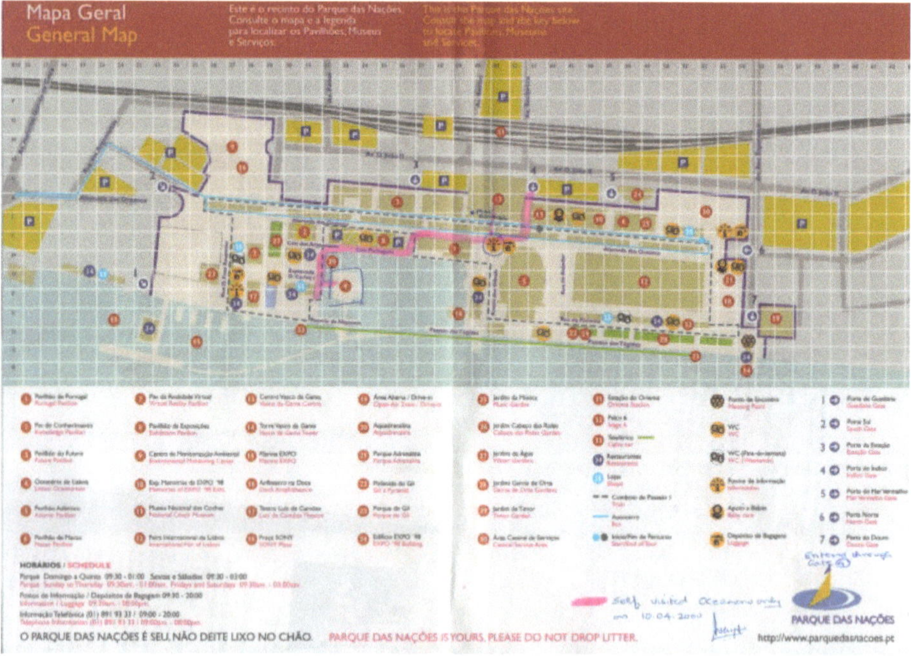

Oceanarium

Porto de Lisboa (38°42'N; 09°11'W) with a population of 2 million is the capital city and the principal port of Portugal. It is situated on the northern bank of the Rio Tejo (Tagus River), about 11 kilometres from its mouth.

The foundation of the port is attributed to the Phoenicians, who, in 1200 BC, gave it the name 'calm harbour'. Rio Tejo rises in the Sierra Molino near Albarracin in the Spanish province of Teruel. It flows westwards and opens out above Lisbon into the Mar da Palha, a broad expanse of water, before entering the sea through a channel one and a half kilometres wide and 13 kilometres long. The river is 772 kilometres long.

The city of Lisbon rises from the north bank of the river in a dense mass of buildings occupying the Southern slopes of a succession of hills. The new part of the city is built on the site of the suburbs which were destroyed by an earthquake in 1755. Estrêla, a church with a conspicuous dome and 2 towers, overlooks the city from the high ground on the west, and Castelo de Sâo Jorge, 2 kilometres to the east, forms the eastern boundary.

Ponte 25 de Abril, a conspicuous suspension bridge, spans the river 10 and a half kilometres from the entrance. The bridge is supported by 2 main pillars, each 190 metres in height, spaced 1000 metres apart, providing a vertical clearance of 70 metres under the central span. Some landmarks as we approached Lisbon from the sea were:

Torre de Belém

Cristo Rei Monument in the distance

Torre de Belém is a conspicuous two-storey tower, 26 metres in height on the North Bank of the river.

Lisbon's Ex Libris is a masterpiece of military architecture in the Manueline style by 16th-century architect Francisco Arruda. It is a UNESCO World Heritage building.

Monumento Dos Descobrimentos Is a Prominent Yellow Stone Monument Standing at the Western Entrance to Doca de Belém. It Was Built in 1960 to Commemorate the 500th Anniversary of the Death of Prince Henry, the Navigator, Promoter of the Discoveries.

Cristo Rei Monument

A 110-metre-high figure of Jesus Christ, standing with outstretched arms on the Southern bank of the 25th April Bridge, is illuminated at night and is a wonderful sight.

A few hundred kilometres to the north, along the coast, lies *Porto*, another port, which is famous for Port Wine. This is a delightful blend of Brandy and Wine, which was/is very popular in Britain and through them among the aristocracy in pre-Independence India. Wine from Europe was being exported to England through Porto. There were complaints of the grape juice getting spoilt. To prevent this, the Portuguese poured a layer of Brandy on top in the cask. The British loved the wine and since it came from Porto, called it Port Wine!

Also famous are almond sweets, sugar-coated almonds in white, pale pink, and now also in pale blue. They look like bird's eggs. They are of sentimental value to me because they were my dad's favourite.

Part 2

SAILING AFRICAN SECTOR

Some people call Africa the dark continent. The Garden of Eden, the beginning of man, Dinosaur land—it all started from here. So why have they not kept pace with the rest of the world?

One needs to understand the African way of thinking, which in many ways is different from the rest of the world. Other societies are driven by caste, religion, the need to excel, or whatever. In Africa, it is the tribe. On special occasions, an African is expected to invite all his near and dear ones. They stay in his house for weeks together, and when they depart, the host is supposed to ply them with gifts and thank them profusely. An African who gains wealth is expected to share it with his tribesmen. The society remains uniformly poor, and there is no motivation to amass wealth. On the contrary, in Western culture, a man who makes money is at liberty to enjoy it all by himself, even to the point of excluding his parents, brothers, and sisters. Since the individual benefits, society is competitive and it advances. People come under a lot of stress and have psychological problems. The African is not under so much stress, and though society does not progress rapidly, the individual is relatively laid back.

Among some of the people I saw ashore, I observed that some of them had scars on their faces, the Shipchandler's driver, for example. It is tradition to carve identifying marks of a tribe on a young boy's face. This remains for life, and a knowledgeable person can immediately say from which tribe the man is by studying the cuts on his face.

Another subject I found intriguing was the face masks. There is such an array of masks, mostly carved out of wood, for the tourists I suspect, but also made of pith. Each mask is of special significance. By looking at a mask, you can tell from which region it has come and what it is used for—a bountiful harvest, victory in war, health, fertility, rain, and so on.

I was fascinated by a palm-sized mask called a Passport Mask. Travellers carried it with them and whenever they were stopped, showing this mask gave them free passage. It really was a passport!

I am told that there are countless languages in Africa. Apparently, each region or tribe has its own language. The amazing thing is that there is no script for many of these languages. So they are only spoken, not written. I should have been born an African. Then I would never have had to listen to complaints about my handwriting!

It is perhaps the saddest part of Africa because it is a continent that has not been fully documented. I could find no books about masks, tribes, or languages.

All the pioneering nations (English, French, German) have divided the continent among themselves, but the African seems not to honour these boundaries, for he roams where he pleases. We get stowaways from Rwanda, Chad, and Zaire, and they all seem to be travelling freely without documentation or visas.

The Africans are not farmers. Their food is cassava, banana, pineapple, and so on, most of which grow wild, I suspect. I have been to a restaurant, which offered monkeys, porcupines, gazelles, jungle rats, etc. So no organised cattle or sheep farming or poultry. I think the underlying thought is that what is nature belongs to everyone, similar to a tribe living in the jungle and just taking what it wants. The concerned people on the ship (captain, chief officer, radio officer, and stewards) all feel that this attitude of take overflows into public life. Take it, even if it is not yours!

The man on the street was very superstitious. He seemed to genuinely believe in Voodoo Magic. We were surprised at the alarm caused when the second officer told one of the stevedores that he knew black magic and that he would put a spell on him.

Sailing ships of old did not have any way of converting seawater to freshwater. Nor could they refrigerate food. So they had to make frequent stops to collect fresh food and water.

Along the African coast, the ships would sign treaties with the local chiefs and these places developed into colonies. The French, through their Communaute Financiere Africaine (CFA), introduced the Central African Franc and the West African Franc as currency.

SENEGAL

REPUBLIC OF SENEGAL

The Republic of Senegal is bounded in the north by Fleuve Senegal, on the east by the Republic of Mali, and on the south by the Republic of Guinea. The Republic of Gambia lies on the banks of the River Gambia in the middle of Senegal. On the northwest coast of Africa, it extends out into the Atlantic more than any other mainland African country.

The Republic has an area of 201,537 square kilometres and a population of 18 million.

History

The Senegal Coast was discovered by the French in the 14th century. The town of Saint Louis was founded in 1659, but it wasn't until the early part of the 18th century that other settlements were established. Until independence in 1960, Senegal has always been a French colony except briefly for a period from 1758 to 1814 when it was occupied by the British.

The inhabitants are composed of Moors and Fulas who are nomadic and pastoral people. Negro races occupy the coastal regions. Of the African races, the main tribe is the Oulofs, who live mostly between Saint Louis and the Gambia. They are physically well-built and hardworking. Over 90% of the population is Muslim.

The French language is used almost throughout the country. The most widely spoken language is Wolof.

Geography

Most of Senegal is flat, dry, and featureless and lies less than 100 metres above sea level. The dry season is between December and May.

There are several large rivers flowing through Senegal:
a) Fleuve Sénégal
b) Rivière Saloum
c) Rivière Casamance

Agriculture forms a large part of the country's economy. Groundnuts, millet, maize and rice are cultivated. Large numbers of sheep, goats, cattle, pigs, horses and camels are reared.

Phosphate rock and iron ore are mined. The country imports petroleum products, cement, and textiles.

Peanuts, peanut products, phosphates, and salt are the main exports.

The CFA (Communauté Financière Africaine) West is the local currency.

Senegal has one of the finest transportation systems in West Africa, and Dakar, the capital, is one of the continent's busiest ports. However, Senegal is not prosperous, and poverty is widespread.

Dakar (14°40'N; 17°26'W)

Dakar is the capital city of Senegal, with a population of 3.5 million. As our ship approached, we passed the island of Goree, which is of volcanic origin and is composed of black basalt, sand, and red and yellow rocks. The south side is about 38 metres high and is nearly vertical with a castle on top. A low, round fort stands on the north end of the island. On the northeastern side was a boat pier.

The island is surrounded by large blocks of stone, and the swell breaks heavily all around the island. The island was used as a penal colony but is now a tourist attraction and has many restaurants.

In my youth, Dakar was considered the *Pearl of West Africa* and we would tune in to Radio Dakar to listen to good music.

The Paris-Dakar car rally is quite famous and it still continues. When we berthed in the morning of 26th January, we saw an assortment of cars and trucks lined up on the pier, all waiting to be shipped back to Le Havre/Paris.

The cars were going back on one ship (Car carrier) belonging to Grimaldi Lines of Italy. Mr. Mark, an Englishman and the local representative of Grimaldi, and Mr. Abdul, the local agent, visited us and had lunch with us. The central subject of our chat was the recently concluded car rally.

The shipper of the rally cars was very particular about advertising rights. The company that was shipping the cars was not permitted to use the fact to advertise its company. The Paris – Dakar rally is a gruelling one across the Sahara Desert and with no air conditioning in the car, it is not easy. Now motorcycles are also allowed to participate in the race.

Earlier, I mentioned trucks. Let us say a team fields 3 cars. This group will be followed by a team truck that carries all repair facilities as well as spares imaginable for the team's cars. Fully loaded, the trucks can weigh up to 30 tons and follow the cars all along the rally route.

The story goes that a rider on a motorcycle was running first. Some person's car had broken down, and he thumbed down the motorcycle rider for help, but the latter refused to stop. The motorcyclist was penalised 1.5 hours for refusing to help a person in trouble. A lady, also on a motorcycle, was declared the winner.

Abdul stressed that he is an educated man. He tells of his friend who did a thesis at Madras University. There is an African language called Pular, which is understood across all of Africa—Kenya, South Africa, everywhere. The thesis proved that Tamil and Pular have the same origin. We also discussed similar food habits. Being Tamil myself, I may please be excused for adding this trivia.

Senegal is famous for tapestries (wall curtains), and we decided to buy some when we went ashore. It was probably the influence of the Moors, who are quite well-known for this industry.

There is an international airport at Yoff, near Dakar.

REPUBLIC OF IVORY COAST

The Republic of Ivory Coast borders the Republics of Liberia and Guinea to the West, Mali and Burkina Faso to the north, and Ghana to the east. The country occupies an area of 322,500 square kilometres and has a population of 30 million. Of this, 5.9 million live in the port city of Abidjan. The capital is Yamoussoukro, 250 kilometres to the north of Abidjan.

Between 1787 and 1868, land tracts were acquired by the French through treaties with the Chiefs on the Ivory Coast, but it was not until 1888 that the land was explored and a protectorate declared in 1891. In 1904, the colony was incorporated into the Government General of French West Africa. The country was proclaimed a republic within the French community in December 1958. Independence was proclaimed in August 1960. Special arrangements with France, covering financial and cultural matters, technical assistance, and defence, were made in April 1961.

The unit of currency is the Franc (CFA) West.

CFA West

There are more than 60 different tribes, of which the most influential are the Baoules in the centre of the country around the city of Bouake, 300 kilometres north of Abidjan.

There are 5 principal language groups, and though French is used exclusively, English is becoming popular as well.

The coast to the west is high and rocky, and immediately behind it, the country rises gradually to the interior. To the east, the region is low and sandy, and behind the coast are a series of lagoons that extend some distance inland. The northern shores of these lagoons are steep and rise to the interior. The country has a 40% forest cover. The main rivers are:

1. Rivière Cavally

2. Rivière Sassandra

3. Rivière Bandama

4. Rivière Comoe

To the south, there are equatorial rainforests, but the climate is drier towards the savannah belt in the north.

Flora and Fauna

Oil palm, rubber, and timber are grown. The country is rich in fauna with various tiger cats, panthers, and lions. Hippopotamuses, bison, and elephants also abound, as are antelopes and monkeys. There are various species of birds. Snakes abound, and in the estuaries, crocodiles are plentiful.

Offshore oil fields discovered in 1977 and 1980 have made the Ivory Coast an oil exporter.

The country is the largest producer of cocoa in the world and, together with coffee, timber, bananas, and pineapple, these products form the bulk of agricultural exports.

ABIDJAN (5°19'N; 4°01'W)

Abidjan is the major port of the Ivory Coast and lies in the Lagune d'Abidjan (Lagoon of Abidjan). The harbour is entered through *Canal de Vridi*, which has been cut through the beach sand. The canal is about 200 metres wide on the seaward side and about 370 metres for the remainder of the length.

The south end of Abidjan is connected to Treichville (the western part to Ile de Petit Bassam) by Pont Houphouet Boigny—a road and railway bridge and also by the road bridge, Pont Charles De Gaulle.

Canal de Vridi and to the right the Beach

Crossing a sister ship at Sea

Canal de Petit Bassam, which divides the island east of Treichville, is spanned by 2 railway and 2 roadway bridges.

The monsoons in Abidjan on the south coast are from May to July. There is a less intense rainy season from October to the end of November.

Port Bouët, an international airport, is about 14 kilometres from Abidjan. Domestic services to Tabou, San Pedro, and Sassandra are also operational from this airport.

I enjoy our visits to Abidjan.

The Third Engineer's Strange Allergy

The third engineer was one Rajendran who joined with me at Ravenna.

After leaving Pointe-Noire (Congo), he complained of a body rash. It was not really a rash, but swellings like insect bites. The rash would appear around 2400 hrs (midnight) and disappear around 1800 hrs the next evening.

Everyone on board assumed it was some allergy. The previous day, Cookie had prepared some squid, and the Captain complained of nausea after having eaten some of it. So we all assumed it would pass. It didn't. The second engineer inspected Rajendran's cabin and found that water from a leak in the bathroom bulkhead was going under the mattress. The wood was being eaten away. So they changed the bunk and fumigated the cabin. Nada. Nothing. The rash continued making its mysterious appearance every midnight.

One evening we were in the smoke room watching a movie when Rajendran suddenly appeared at the doorway with a panicked expression on his face, complaining of intense stomach ache. After deliberations, he was given ENO fruit salt, and he recovered from the stomach ache. Was it gas? Rajendran was physically tough, but I believed something was attacking his intestines. Then he started developing fever on and off. The doctor at Douala gave him some antihistamine tablets (anti-allergy) and sent him off. Again, no improvement. At Abidjan, we insisted on a blood test. Rules here are like in Europe. People need to be hospitalised before any tests are done. So into the hospital, Rajendran went, and the blood test showed he had some strange strain of malaria.

The Captain and I visited the hospital. He was given a comfortable room with an attached bath, television, and air conditioning. A glass window ran the length of the room, making it quite bright. Outside the window, there was some shrubbery on which sparrows flitted around. The sparrows here had the same colours as the ones in India, but the hues were much darker, and the colours were, therefore, much more vibrant. The crows, too, were similar to the ones we have in India, but they have a snow-white collar, unlike the grey collar that the Indian crows have.

Back to the patient. The Captain was confident of treating malaria on board, so he wanted to take the third engineer back to the ship before departure. We did not want to leave behind one of our own in a hospital in Africa. The doctor, a white Frenchman, was quite upset, I am told. Fortunately, the ship was delayed and after 2 days, the third engineer was discharged and back on board. On the way out, the doctor told the third engineer that he had determined what had caused the allergy and prescribed some tablets. The third engineer had not bothered to find out. Apparently, language had been a big problem for him because all the nurses and room boys spoke French only. In all other matters, it was a good hospital and I was duly impressed. Not much crowd with just 4 or 5 patients on view in the waiting area, unlike our hospitals in India.

We entered the Port of Abidjan through the approach channel. The entrance was a bit tricky due to cross-currents and the rocks on the breakwater, but the pilot on board lined up the vessel and then went full ahead.

Instances of piracy have been reported at the outer anchorage, so Masters prefer to stop and drift about 24 to 32 kilometres away until the berth is ready.

Some people who have been at the inner anchorage report that people from the surrounding villages approach by boat, and brisk bartering takes place with empty oil drums for fish, pineapple, mango, and prawns.

The port officials are the worst I have ever seen. They demand and take caseloads of beer, soft drinks, cigarettes, and wine. Even minor variations in the customs ship's store declaration can attract ridiculously heavy fines if they decide to rummage. Other port officials also board, and minor infringements can attract heavy fines as per the law, but it is usually negotiable. Thank God we engineers are not exposed to this. The radio officer takes the brunt of it, and sometimes the Captain as well.

We usually berth at Quay 17, and it is a short walk to gate no 4, where one can hail a taxi. Unfortunately, at this point, there are also many roadside bars with unfavourable elements, and a sailor caught here at night is a sitting duck for a mugging. There have been many instances. However, it is quite safe in the daytime. About one dollar (700 CIFA) takes you to the main post office, where the Philatelic Bureau is also located. My business is usually there.

To the right is apparently the industrial part of the city and also the poorer sections. You get across a bridge to reach *Le Plateau*, which is the fashionable part of town. Here live the President, the rich businessmen, the corrupt politicians, and so on.

Another section of town is called *Treichville*. This is the business section where most of the shops are located. Owned mostly by Lebanese, they usually deal in Chinese and Nigerian goods.

At times, the agent has taken us to another part of town called *Cocody* where most of the expats seem to stay. There is a quiet block of about 6 restaurants—Italian, Chinese, Lebanese, etc. On all 3 occasions, we preferred the Italian restaurant for pizza, and I really enjoyed the evenings.

Hotel Côte d'Ivoire International

There is a 5-star hotel, *Hotel Côte d'Ivoire International*. It has one of the most fancy swimming pools I have ever seen. The hotel has everything—a bowling alley, piano bar, discotheque, cinema theatre, and shopping arcade.

The Jamaican Stowaway

A few days after sailing out on a relaxed Sunday, after dinner, we had all assembled in the officers' smoke room to play Tombola. It was Rs. 10.00 per ticket. After 2 rounds of play, the electrical officer, Krishnamoorthy stepped out near the port gangway deck for a smoke. He saw a black guy approaching from Aft, and the fellow fells down and pretended to faint. People rushed out, and the party was disrupted because we had a stowaway on board. Procedures were followed.

The fellow claimed he was well-to-do, having an Automobile Workshop in Jamaica. He gave me an address and the name of his sister! According to him, he came as a tourist to South Africa by air. At Douala, he was robbed of all his money and papers. So he decided to stowaway! Where does he want to go? To Europe. Our principals in the office checked and found that the address he had given in Jamaica was false.

We arrived at Sagunto (Spain) on the 15th evening. Mr. Jim Stout, a short, squat man, ran a company that specialised in the repatriation of stowaways. He came on board with the pilot boat, took photographs of the stowaway, and made a Ghanaian passport! When the officials boarded the vessel, the stowaway insisted he was Jamaican, so Mr. Stout's plan of deporting him fell through. This trick of producing false passports works only with certain countries.

So we were stuck with the fellow and expected that we would have to carry him back to Africa. In Africa, they would take a few cases of beer from the ship, kick the stowaway's butt up to the gate and then turn him loose!

I digress! Let's return to Abidjan! Another place worth a visit is Saint Paul's Cathedral. A very modern white building which, I was told, could seat a congregation of 1000 people. The seating was spacious but more impressive were the excellent stained glass windows.

St. Paul's Cathedral, Abidjan

Ivory Coast stamps are very colourful.

The main post office was in the *Plateau* area, soon after crossing the bridge. En route, we passed a circular building called the *Palais du Sport*. Indoor games such as boxing, basketball, and table tennis were played here.

There is apparently some Indian population around as we have an Indian Embassy. One Mr. Subramaniam was here with his family, and he had become friendly with our radio officer, Satya, and even visited on board. The Embassy staff were all very polite and helpful. We usually got all our passport work done in Abidjan. In fact, my present passport was issued in Abidjan.

The local agency was headed by a rusty old Italian called Giovanni. He was a football player of sorts and played at the age of 60. When I marvelled at his capability, he moaned, "The mind is still fast but the body is slow."

Giovanni once took the Captain and me to a seaside restaurant with his son. We feasted on prawns, fish, and wine. The son was doing graduation in Paris where his father had set him up in an apartment. Giovanni himself had been working around in the West African region for 30 years. He took us to his home once. It was palatial with a swimming pool and so on! We also met Mrs. Giovanni and though she was nice, you could see she was washed out. Life in Africa must be tough for her!

Giovanni's assistant was one Simone. He had accompanied us a couple of times for a meal at Cocody and once to an African eating area. At the time of writing, the company is grooming another young Italian called Giorgio to step into Giovanni's shoes. Giorgio's father is big in the timber export business from Douala. At times he complains about Africa, but he has a car, apartment, dog, mobile phone, and the support of the Italian community, even from Ravenna.

The *Oisseau Bleu* was a bar-cum-restaurant being run by a Spanish family from their home. An outhouse had been converted into a crude dance floor with a bar. One part of the house (2 rooms) served as a seating area, and a patio served as a bar cum cash register. I believe it is quite popular in the evenings, but I only went for lunch.

Some political unrest in the country while we were away in Europe which has led to 2000 people already dying in the shootings. There was a curfew in the city from 2000 hrs to 0600 hrs.

Soldiers who had been given 1.5 years of military training had been disbanded and sent home some years ago. They were demanding permanent employment, but this could not be arranged immediately. Some friction and an unhappy lot went and settled in nearby Burkina Faso some years ago. This was common as there were many people from Burkina Faso living in Ivory Coast.

The Ivorians wanted to build a second bridge in Abidjan. A French company quoted for it. The President approached the Chinese and Japanese for quotations as well, and they were half of what the French had quoted. The contract was about to be given to them, which the French did not like. So they stirred up the unhappy soldiers in Burkina Faso. They also floated a rumour that the President was against the people of Burkina Faso and was planning to deport them from the Ivory Coast.

So the rebellion!

Port operations were slow, so we had to wait for 3 days at the anchorage.

While alongside at Abidjan, we saw a security guard with a dog. We asked him if Max, the ship's dog, could be allowed to mate with the bitch. The guard demanded $10.00. Some haggling followed, with our radio officer going on about Max's superior pedigree and the guard deriding Max, saying he was too big and fat. It came down to $6.00, and Max barked gleefully at the prospect of losing his virginity. The lady, however, was not in the mood, and she bared her fangs, so Max had to beat a hasty retreat. Poor Max looked glum the next day, and all on board were feeling sad for him.

Have to leave Max now, but I will tell you more about him later.

We went ashore with one of the ship's drivers, Theodore*, and the Deck Cadet. We engaged shore drivers to operate the forklifts, and they sailed with us on the African leg.

First, I went to the post office at Treichville and then to the internet centre at *Cape Sud*. The taxi fare from the gate (Porte 4, Quai dix-sept) across the bridge was about a dollar (700 CIFA).

Cape Sud was the new shopping mall in Abidjan, located in the Marcory area. Very upper class and mostly expats and the rich locals used it. It occupied 2 storeys with a car park in front and elevators in the building. The internet centre was here. Charges for browsing were 500 CIFA for 15 minutes. Expensive!

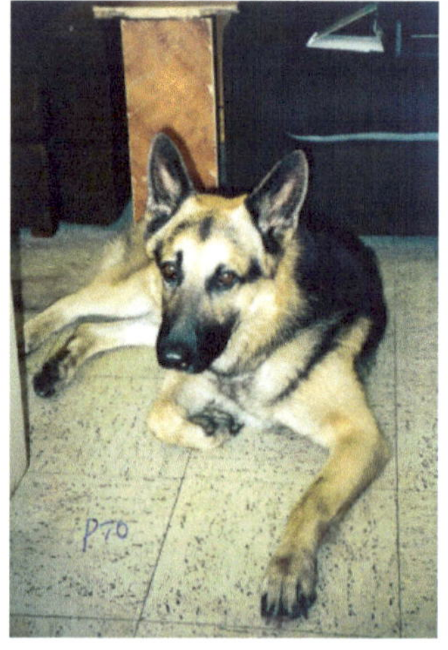

Max, the ship's mascot

Back at the gate, Theodore wanted to go for an African lunch instead of the Indian food on board. Bijoy needed to return to the ship as he went on duty soon. I decided to try the authentic African lunch for a change.

Outside the main gate of the harbour were 2 rows of about 50 restaurants. They catered lunch for the people working in the port and nearby offices.

The restaurant we chose had a tin sheet roof. The entrance was bisected by a big table, which acted as the cashier's desk and the food service area. The food was kept in big vessels. Inside, there were 2 crude wooden tables with plastic tablecloths and benches seating 8 people. It had another table against the back wall. This was stacked high with crates of Heineken Beer, Coke, Sprite, bottles of Whisky, and Guinness Stout. Under the table, a small child slept in spite of all the din.

We found 2 places and sat opposite each other. I ordered cassava and Theodore ordered the rest. The last time I had cassava, it was grated like coconut, but here it has been powdered and boiled till it is thick like dough (that is used for bread). Two cupfuls were served on a plate. There was fish curry served in a mud *chatti* (pan) that had become black with age. There was a complete fish, about 10 inches long; it was fresh and tasted good. The curry was excellent—a thick gravy that was a little pungent. You take spoonfuls of cassava, dip it in the fish curry and eat. Cutlery was handed out and at Theodore's request, a napkin was provided for me. Drinking water was served in big plastic mugs, but I was afraid to drink it.

Theodore had rice and fish curry with a big headpiece. Everyone seemed to be having the same, so the choice was limited, I guess. The atmosphere was not elegant, but the people were polite with *Excusez Moi* and *Bon Appetit*. They may be poor, but their manners were in place.

A middle-aged lady filled out the food at the front table and handled the cash while 3 young girls served. Like most African girls, they were dressed in tight tops and tight skirts, displaying their ample figures.

At night, the girls cleaned up and the booze that was stacked at the back was moved up front, and the place became a bar for shippies who were brave enough to venture out. It was an enjoyable experience, lunching out in Abidjan!

Main Post Office

View from the main post office, Abidjan

Tchamawa seller

Chi Chi was an illegal telephone operator who used to come on board ships in port and she used to sell a regular lunch.

The locals (in Abidjan) call it *Tchamawa*. The bread crust is hard, but the inside is quite soft. It is slit open at the side, and the meat (beef) pieces are put inside with chopped onion. Quite tasty and filling! Chi Chi, later on, took to ship chandling, and when I last heard, she was doing quite well.

The Republic of Benin, formerly known as Dahomey, is bordered on the west by the Republic of Togo, on the north by the Republic of Upper Volta and Niger, and on the east by the Republic of Nigeria.

The country has a total area of 112,620 square kilometres and a population of about 13 million. Porto-Novo is the capital city, and Cotonou is the only seaport.

The main rivers in this country are the River Niger in the north and the Fleuve Mono and Oume Fleuve in the south.

Benin's main imports are textiles and general cargo. It exports palm oil kernels, cotton, groundnuts, coconuts, and tobacco.

History

The Portuguese established a trading post at Porto-Novo. At that time, the territory was a collection of small states owing allegiance to the Kingdom of Dahomey to the north. This kingdom had been pushing against the Yorubas and other coastal tribes since the 16th century.

The French obtained a footing on the coast in 1851 and through treaties gradually extended their power until 1894, when the whole Kingdom of Dahomey was annexed. The Republic of Dahomey became independent in 1958, and full independence was proclaimed in August 1960.

In 1963, the army took over the government. After several coups and changes in political regime, the country's name was changed to the People's Republic of Benin on 30th November 1975.

The population of the country comprises more than 40 ethnic groups, with the 4 main groups being the Fos, the Adjas, the Yorubas, and the Baribas.

French is the official language, but about 47% of the people speak Fon, 23% speak Adja, 10% speak Bariba, and 9% speak Yoruba.

Cotonou, the port for Porto-Novo, lies 24 kilometres east-northeast and is the only port for the Republic of Benin. It is a large and well-sheltered artificial harbour, close to the mouth of Lake Nokoue.

This was my first visit to the Republic of Benin, and I was delighted to have the opportunity of going ashore. The electrical officer and I went together.

Going ashore by Taxi

Main Street

At the main gate, we searched for a pilot and he came up with 2 motorcycles—small TVS 50-sized ones. It was about a 10-minute ride into town.

The town had one main street on which you had everything. The main street was a well-paved, double road with a lot of traffic.

American Influence

Shopping on Main Street

There were some fine new cars and the people were well-dressed. The main street had a Telegraph Office with an internet centre, a big bookshop, a department store, and some other bigger shops. Main Street is about 2 kilometres long. The Cotonou skyline is dominated by a 10-storey bank building on Main Street that is illuminated at night.

On the pavements along Main Street were shops selling suitcases, and compact discs, and roving salesmen selling watches, belts, and sunglasses. There were a few shops selling stationery, picture postcards, and such. The best restaurant in town is called *Titanic*.

The main post office had a Philatelic Bureau, and I was thrilled to buy some stamps and First Day Covers. Stamps of Dahomey were on display but not available for sale.

On a diagonal to Main Street is a shopping mall with many small shops selling electrical and electronic goods, videotapes and CDs (Nigerian products), fruits, and such things. These shops are typical of Africa. In the 'Y' formed between Main Street and the shopping mall is the market where I could see vegetables, fruit, and fresh fish on sale. Very similar to the Saidapet market back home in Chennai. Practically in a ring around Main Street were the restaurants, bars, and nightclubs. Beyond this lay the residential areas. The airport, the harbour, and the small industries occupied the outskirts of the city.

Catholicism is the main religion, but there is a Muslim presence mainly coming from the northern region.

We bought postletters at the main post office, First Day Covers at the Philatelic Bureau, visited the bookshop and bought postcards. The bookshop was fancy and was owned by a Frenchman. The postcards were almost a dollar each. The pilot suggested we buy them from the pavement shops, where they were for half the price.

There was nothing to see or do in Cotonou! It was just an experience—to walk on firm ground, to rub shoulders with strange people, the noise of traffic, different colours, different smells, that's all.

LUANDA, ANGOLA

The People's Republic of Angola is a big country and after Zaire, it is the largest country in Africa. Lying south of the Sahara, it has an area of 1,246,700 square kilometres. Bounded in the north and northeast by Zaire, on the southeast by Zambia, and on the south by Namibia. It has an Atlantic coastline of about 1600 kilometres, including that of the province of Cabinda. Separated from the main part of Angola, Cabinda has an area of 7270 square kilometres, a population of 739,000 and lies in an enclave between the Republics of Congo and Zaire, north of the mouth of the Congo River.

For its size, Angola is sparsely populated with a total of 35.6 million people. The country was overwhelmingly rural and tribal with not more than 11% of the population living in towns with a population of 2000 or more. That has changed now.

I went ashore just once in Luanda, and it was a sad experience. Some rebels were creating a ruckus in the country. To meet their needs, they would raid the small villages in the mountains. Having no place to go, the villagers crowded into the city. They were kept out of the expensive areas, but elsewhere in the city, there was a palpable crush of people doing nothing. The danger of petty crime was constant.

During the entire period that I was ashore, the city had a power cut. Only a few lights with emergency power supply worked.

Angola is a rich country and I hope that by the time I finish writing this book, she regains her past glory.

The principal cities are:
- **Luanda**, the capital city
- **Lobito** is a large and important port.
- **Benguela**, the capital of Benguela District, is a city of historic importance and a leading centre of the fishing industry.
- **Malanje** is the island terminus of the Luanda Railway and stands at an elevation of 1070 metres. It is the centre of a rich agricultural area that produces coffee, sisal, cereals, cotton, tobacco, and beeswax.
- **Huambo** (Nova Lisboa), the designated future capital, lies 240 kilometres inland from Benguela on the Benguela Railway. It is the centre of a large agricultural district.

- **Sa Da Bandeira** is at an elevation of 1760 metres and about 130 kilometres east-northeast of Moçamedes, to which it is connected by railway. It is a centre for trade, agriculture, and cattle raising.
- **Moçamedes**, formerly the main fishing port near the Southwest African border, is now becoming (Porto Salazar), an important port for iron ore exports. It was later named Namibe.

History

The mouth of the River Congo was first known to Europeans by the voyage of Diego Cão in 1485. At the south of the entrance, he erected the first *Padrão* (a stone column surmounted by a Cross), which King João II had ordered to be set up on newly discovered lands.

Angola became a Portuguese dependency in 1574, but it was not until 1597 that serious attempts were made to colonise it. At around 1627, the Queen of Angola waged war against the Portuguese and drove them from Luanda. The Dutch took advantage and moved in. In 1648, however, the Dutch were expelled, and Angola remained a possession of Portugal until its independence on 11th November 1975.

The official language is still Portuguese, but French and Spanish are also understood.

Two-thirds of Angola is a plateau with an average altitude of 1050 to 1350 metres. Therefore, temperatures are generally cooler. The highest peak is Mount Moco (2620 m) in the Huambo District. Other peaks include Mount Mepo (2583m) in the Benguela District and Mount Vavéle (2479m) in the Cuanza Sul district.

The river Rio Cuanza is navigable 193 kilometres upstream, up to Dondo, and plays a major part in opening up the Ngola Kingdom. Other rivers are Cubango, Cuito, and in the north Kwango and Kasai, which are the tributaries of the Congo.

Health

Sleeping sickness has been fairly common along the coast as far south as São Felipe de Benguela. Malaria is prevalent along the coast. Blackwater fever exists. Leprosy in a mild form is rather common. Smallpox has often proved a scourge. Pleurisy and pulmonary diseases are endemic, and a disease known as Katumbu, with symptoms similar to whooping cough, is common among children.

Flora

The coast of Angola is poorly watered and infertile. Rubber-producing plants are commonly found. The plateau, mostly covered by grass, the baobab, African mahogany, and other timber trees are common. In the arid south, the baobab and spiny acacias are common. The other common trees are kapok, fibre, oil palm, and Coffea arabica (coffee, which is native to Angola).

Fauna

Few animals are found on the coast except in river valleys where there are antelope, gazelle, monkeys, and parrots. Sometimes hyenas wander down from the hills. At a slightly higher elevation, leopards, zebras, and elephants are common. Big game is plentiful, and at higher levels, one can find numerous wild pigs and goats. Elephants appear in large numbers in the north and south between Rio Cubango and Rio Cunene. There are some rhinoceroses as well.

Angola is famous for the giant Sable—the antelope with the longest horns of any game animal. Buffalo, antelope, leopards, wolves and jackals are common on the plateau. In the south, Gemsbok roams the Namib Desert in large numbers, as do 2 kinds of zebra.

There are numerous Cape Buffalo along the lowland rivers (Rio Caporolo) and near Luanda. The red dwarf variety or the Bush Cow lives in the swamp. Gnu, Hartebeest, Tsessebe, Eland, and black-faced Impala are other animals which are found.

Hippopotamuses, crocodiles and alligators frequent many of the rivers. Pythons, cobras and other kinds of venomous snakes are common in various parts of the country. The rivers abound in fish, with the Bagre variety being much esteemed as a native food.

The tsetse fly, which causes sleeping sickness, the mosquito, which causes malaria, and the salale or white ant are all found in the lowlands.

National Game Reserves

a)   Parque Nacional de Quiçama - south of Luanda

b)   Parque Nacional da Cameia - in the eastern part of the country, east of Luso

c)   Iona National Park - on the coast, north of Rio Cunene

Chief Produces

Coffee, maize, sugar, palm oil, palm kernel, cotton, wheat, tobacco, cocoa, sisal, wax.

The country has valuable diamond deposits as well as iron ore, copper, and manganese.

Produce of Cabinda includes ivory, oil, gum, wax, and honey. They trade in Gum Copal.

The currency unit is the Angolar, consisting of 100 centavos. One thousand Angolars make up a Conto.

There are 3050 kilometres of railway line. The Benguela railway runs from Porto do Lobito through the Republic of Zaire and Rhodesia and ends at Porto da Beira in Mozambique. Another railway line connects Luanda with Malanje and Dondo.

The airport in Luanda is called the Craveiro Lopes Airport.

Luanda Port

Porto De Luanda is protected on the seaward side by Ilha de Cabo, a low narrow island about 5 and a half kilometre long, joined to the mainland by a bridge. Due to some unknown reason, dead fish are occasionally washed up in large quantities on the northeast bank of Ilha de Cabo.

LIBREVILLE, REPUBLIC OF GABON

Formerly a French colony, it became independent on 17 August 1960, having previously been one of the 4 territories of French Equatorial Africa and from 1958, a member of the French Community.

Located astride the equator, it has an area of 267,000 square kilometres and comprises the entire drainage basin of Fleuve Ogooue, which is one of the great rivers of Africa; it is over 885 kilometres long. The Ogooue rises in the Republic of Congo, near Zanaga, bisects Gabon and enters the sea in a large delta around Cap Lopez. Much of the country is covered with dense equatorial forests, and there is heavy rainfall. Mont du Chaillu rises to an elevation of 1190 metres in the south of the country, 322 kilometres inland.

The inhabitants are of Bantu stock, and the total population is 2.39 million, of which some are of European origin.

The capital is Libreville, and other towns are Port Gentil and Lambarene. The country is bounded in the north by Rio Muni (Province of Equatorial Guinea), by Cameroon on the east, and in the south by Congo.

French is the official language.

The country is rich in minerals, including manganese and uranium. There are numerous deposits of high-grade iron ore. Mining started in the mid-1970s at the Belinga Mines. Railway tracks are being laid for a new port at Owendo (on Rivière Gabon), which will connect to the big mining centre at Moanda.

Malaria is prevalent. Bilious fevers are common. Sleeping sickness exists in certain districts.

The Franc CFA (Central) is the currency unit. Roads connect Libreville, Lambarene, Brazzaville, Pointe-Noire and also Yaoundé (Cameroon). There are large airports at Libreville and Port Gentil.

We berthed at the new port of Owendo. It is a short walk to the gate, but one needs to catch transport for the 40-minute drive to the city of Libreville.

Privately owned 20-seater vans and shared taxis are available at the gate and charge 500 CIFA (about a dollar) one way, which is very reasonable.

I have been to the post office twice before to visit the Philatelic Bureau. I went for dinner with Captain S* and his wife to a place called Shalimar Restaurant, and once, an agent took Captain V* and me for lunch.

View of Libreville Port

Shalimar, at the other end of town, was run by a Sindhi who was operating out of Las Palmas and somehow landed up here. His wife is Goan/Mangalorean from Poona. Captain N* and I first picked up Captain and Mrs. S* from their apartment and then met up with the agent and his wife at the restaurant. The agent's wife worked for an agency that handled Indian ships, so she was familiar with Indians but she hardly spoke any English. Although it was an Indian restaurant, the food was hardly Indian. Fried rice and a general curry with prawns and so on, but the company was good and we enjoyed the evening. The next day the family visited the ship with their daughters.

Another memorable outing was when a chandler took Capt V*, the agent, and myself for lunch at a local restaurant. A lady in a clean white dress waited on us. The menu surprised me! Jungle rats, gazelle, porcupines, and monkeys were part of it!

I went to Gazelle, expecting something fantastic, but these fellows are very poor cooks. The dish was pieces of meat boiled in water, without many spices. So it was a tasteless, rubbery affair! Capt V* went for the wild boar, and he did not fare any better!

While one part of the world screams for conservation, these fellows are happily chopping up all these jungle animals. I believe there is enough to go around.

After lunch, we visited the agent's home. His family was not around, so we did not get to meet them. He had a most impressive collection of wooden curios. He also had a large (3'x2') collage made up of butterfly wings, which he presented to us.

DOUALA, UNITED REPUBLIC OF CAMEROUN (4°03'N; 9°41'E)

Joining Kwanza

left home to catch the 0900 (Jet Airways) flight to Mumbai. Checked in baggage at Hotel Accord and took the same taxi into town. There was a lot of activity in the office as we were buying this ship, and crew selection was going on. The Captain was already on board as an observer, and I was to join him at Douala.

I was to fly by Swissair from Bombay to Zurich, and then to Malabo and Douala. I was expected to arrive at 2000 hrs local time. Agent Mr. King met me and took me to Hotel Falaise.

The ship arrived the next day but was delayed at the anchorage. I shifted to the Seamen's Club on the 28th at noon. The ship berthed on the 29th morning!

The Kwanza is what we call a roll-on/roll-off carrier. She does not need cranes to load or discharge cargo. Instead, she has a huge ramp at the back, and all cargo that is on wheels is simply driven on or off the ship.

At that time, she was operating on a regular run between Mediterranean and West African ports.

I arrived at the ship with bags and baggage only to be greeted by a huge, snarling German Shepherd at the entrance. Fortunately, the dog was chained and could not physically attack me.

Shortly, the Duty Officer arrived and took him away, and I was able to pass through. I went up to the Captain's cabin, presented my papers, and was officially welcomed on board.

After exchanging pleasantries, I mentioned the warm welcome I received at the entrance.

"Ah, you have met Max!" the Captain said.

The next morning, I go to the Captain's cabin. He called up the Duty Officer on his walkie-talkie (two-way radio) and asked him to bring Max up to his cabin. A few minutes later, the second officer walks in with Max on a leash.

On seeing me, Max starts to growl. The Captain gave me 2 biscuits to hold onto. He kept stroking Max and saying to him, "Friend! Friend! Friend." The growling subsided but Max continued to stare at me as he sized me up.

"Shake hands, Max!" the Captain commanded.

After a while, I was pleasantly surprised; no, I was amazed to see Max put forward his right paw! We shook hands. Then I gave him the 2 biscuits, which he graciously ate. I was allowed to stroke him, which I gingerly did. That's it! The introductions were over, and Max and I were now friends.

The African Arrow presently has a Greek Captain, all Bulgarian Officers, and a Filipino crew. The food was nice, for a change, but I got fed up with it after a while. For breakfast, it was eggs (cook's choice) and some cold meat. You have to serve yourself toast, cornflakes, and coffee. For both lunch and dinner, there is an entree on the table and a selection of fruit—orange, banana, apple. At lunchtime, we would have spaghetti as the first plate, beef steak with boiled peas and carrots as the second plate, and a beer or a soft drink to go with it. For dinner, perhaps fried fish or chicken with potato chips. Sometimes we were served ice cream at night.

The African Arrow is a large, dark blue ship with 5 open decks for cargo and serviced by a cargo elevator. I digress to give the technical buffs some numbers. Area-wise, the cargo space can hold 1900 cars (1500 TEU). Another 5 decks make up the superstructure and are served by another domestic lift. At 26,800 BHP/20 knots, she is the most powerful and fastest ship I have ever served on. The main engine is a SULZER 8RND90M with 3 turbochargers and 2 x 1500 kW and 2 x 1000 kW Crepelle generators.

Douala Port,

Cameroon M.V. Kwanza

The Kwanza was doing a run that was ideal for stowaways seeking free passage from Africa to Europe. They smuggled themselves onto the ship during cargo operations and remained in hiding on the ship until we reached Europe. There they made a bid to escape. If caught, they were returned to the ship and then became a nightmare for the ship's crew as they had to be constrained. They were usually kept locked in a cabin and fed 3 meals a day. They did not carry identification papers of any sort, so no country would accept them and putting them ashore became a difficult proposition.

Before leaving the last African port for Europe, the ship's crew carried out a stowaway search. Guard dogs were also trained for stowaway searches, and Max was an expert at his job.

It has been some years since Max and I sailed as shipmates, but I can never forget him. Max was kept on a leash only when the ship was in port. Once we were out at sea, Max was set free and then had full access to any place on the ship. Each morning, around 1000 hrs, Max would stick his head into my cabin door with his pointed ears and wolfish smile. He would enter only if I invited him with a "Come in, Max!" He would then hang around, spending some time with me before moving on. The journey—from the way he first welcomed me on board to becoming friends and then going on to become good friends—was amazing. The ship's crew is regularly changing with people going on leave and new faces joining. The skill to identify newcomers is one that I thought only humans possessed. Max taught me otherwise.

Cameroon is bounded by Nigeria to the west, Chad to the east, and Congo and Gabon to the south. The total area is 490,000 square kilometre and the population is 13.13 million.

Yaoundé is the capital city and has a population of 850,000. It is the centre for the export of timber, cocoa, coffee, and vegetable oils.

The country is bilingual, as French and English are widely spoken. There is no distinct account of when it was discovered by the Europeans,

My Cabin on board

but it is presumed to be in 1471. The name, derived from the Portuguese *Camaroes* or Prawns, was certainly bestowed by early explorers from Portugal.

An English Baptist Mission was established in 1845, and in 1853, the same mission also settled in Victoria, now Limbe. It was visited by European merchants and missionaries until it was declared a German Protectorate by Nachtigal on 12 July 1884.

On 18 February 1916, the territory was taken over by the British and French troops with the greater portion being placed under the French and the remainder under the British. The latter portion consisted of 2 parts, and at a plebiscite held in February 1961, the north joined Nigeria and the south joined Cameroon, which was declared a republic on 01 October 1961. The south included Buea (the Capital) and the Ports of Victoria and Tiko.

A national referendum was held on 20 May 1972 and on 02 June 1972, and the unitary, bilingual, and pluricultural state came into force as the United Republic of Cameroon.

Former occupying powers/discoverers called it by various names:

Camaroňes (Spanish), Kamerun (German), Cameroun (French), and Cameroon (English).

Flora

There are mangrove swamps along the greater part of the coast, extending 31 kilometres inland. Pandanus and Raffia palms grow on the lowlands and higher up, forests of large trees are matted together by a tangled network of tall creepers.

Beyond, the plateau is covered by high, reedy, and hard grass. The cultivated plants are coconut, oil palm, banana, yams, groundnuts, sweet potato, cassava, and especially colocasia and also coffee, cocoa, rubber, and kola.

Fauna

Wild boars are commonly found in the marshlands along with pelicans, herons, snipe, and other birds.

In the large rivers, there are hippopotamuses, crocodiles, tortoises, and crabs, and on the banks, there are snakes.

Flowers from Africa

In the forest, herds of elephants, antelope, and buffalo exist. Monkeys, squirrels, and pigs are to be found. Guinea fowl, pheasants, and also mosquitoes, sand flies, and ants abound.

The rivers are full of fish, many of which are good to eat; one among them is the Nile Perch. Every fourth year in August/September, the Cameroon River and neighbouring estuaries swarm with little yellowish shrimp, so closely packed that they are caught in baskets.

A great movement of people has occurred in Cameroon, and the distribution of race and tribe is a complicated problem. The bulk of the population consists of Sudanese and Bantu Negros. The geographic line that divides them is fairly close to the north Savannah and the South Forest country.

Bantu languages are much more closely related than those of Sudanese Negroes. The older group of Bantu falls into the Bakoko and Bakundu in the Southwest, and the Maka in the southeast. The younger group intervenes between the 2 sections and consists of the Fang group. The Bangala language is widely spoken.

The Sudanese tribes are related very obscurely, and their languages are different. They are usually found south of Lake Chad. Some large tribes live in the open plains and highlands, while others have been driven into inaccessible parts of the mountains.

The Pygmies share the forest region with the Bantus. These people are called Bagielli, Babinga, Bumanjok, and Bomassa in various places. Their numbers are small and decreasing. Little is known about their language.

After the Bantu and the Sudanese tribes, the most important are the Fulbe and Hausa.

The country principally exports cocoa, palm kernels, timber, coffee, bananas, groundnuts, and rubber and imports transport equipment, agricultural, and industrial machinery, consumer products, food, drink, and tobacco.

The Central CFA (Communauté Financière Africaine) is used as currency.

CFA Central

The population comprises mostly Christians in the west and south and Muslims in the centre and north. Cameroonian Railways link Douala with Nkongsamba and Belabo with M'bangakumba and Makak-M'Balmayo. Belabo is also now connected to Ngaoundere.

Cameroon has a network of 40,000 kilometres of road, of which only 1,500 kilometres are tarred, and more than half are merely tracks. Yaoundé is connected by road to Douala, Buea, and Nigeria. Bongin connects Libreville, Lambarene, and Pointe-Noire.

The city has a population of 27.9 million and is situated on elevated ground, about 9 metres above River Wouri. The town is divided by a railway cutting, the southwest part being known as Bell and the northeast as Akwa. A bridge connects the 2. Another bridge connects the town with Bonaberi on the west side of the river.

Douala is connected by rail to Yaoundé, which is about 300 kilometres away. From Bonaberi, another line runs to Nkongsamba, which is about 120 kilometres away. Roads connect Douala, Bonaberi, Nkongsamba, and Bafoussam.

In 1984, the country was renamed the Republic of Cameroon and comprised of 10 provinces, each with its own governor. It was further divided into divisions and subdivisions.

Armed men boarded a ship in Douala in July 1991 in the first recorded act of piracy here.

Timber stockyard in Douala Port

Container Terminal in Douala Port

The Kwanza calls regularly at Douala. On one of our visits, just 5 ship lengths away from us, was a famous ship, the Doulos. Built in 1914, she is the oldest ocean-going passenger ship in the world. There were 350 people on board from 40 different countries.

M.V. DOULOS

On the pier, I meet Jacob* from India and invite him for lunch. He came with his friend Danendran*, both from Kerala. They enjoyed the fish curry and rice as they had a British chef on board and he served them the bland stuff.

Later in the evening, the electrical officer and I visited Jacob. He was kind enough to take us around the mess room, the conference room, and down to the engine room.

I was looking forward to seeing some ancient machinery, but there were retrofits. We saw the third main engine for the ship—a 1970-built FIAT engine running at 450 rpm. A surprising retrofit, considering the first main engine was a steam engine! Electricity has been changed over from DC to AC, and a lot of machinery was new. The only original equipment, we were told, was the propeller and the propeller shaft. There was a book exhibition being held on the quarterdeck, which was overcrowded, and one had to wait for hours in the queue to pay.

Because of our regular calls to Douala, I also made good friends with the pastor, Carl* and his wife Elke*, who are presently running the German Seaman's Mission in Douala. They picked me up from the ship at 0745 hrs in their Seaman's Mission van. Since it was a Sunday, we are going to church. We went in a white Mitsubishi van that seated 10 plus 2. A sticker on the side said that it was donated by the ITF (International Transport Workers Federation).

Other than me, Rick* was there with his German girlfriend. I didn't catch her name and did not bother to find out. Rick was an American. Born in Ohio State, his parents moved to Florida for the warmer climate. He was tall, a little over 6 feet, and was simply dressed in a cotton shirt, pants, and open sandals. I could pick his strong American accent.

Rick worked for about 6 years with animals in Florida. For the past 3 years, he has been in Africa, looking after the Zoo at Limbe, a tourist beach resort some 100 kilometres away. The Zoo was in a run-down condition, but Rick said it was improved now, and they had 9 gorillas and 14 chimpanzees. Money (funding) seemed to be the problem as Rick was inquiring about getting back to the USA by boat as it was cheaper. "They don't pay me enough to afford an airline ticket," he said ruefully.

"Have you had any scary experiences in Africa?" I asked.

He told me about the time he went swimming in a lake that was supposed to be safe when, quite suddenly, a hippopotamus took him around the waist and dragged him underwater. It shook him this way and that, and then, for some strange reason, let him go.

"I'm lucky to be alive because a hippo usually does not pass up a good meal," he said.

Rick offered to show me the scars, but I was hardly in the mood for a male striptease in the church compound!

Except for a brief handshake, the German girl and I had not spoken. She was dressed in the same loose cotton pants, a t-shirt, and open sandals. He had short brown hair and a Plain Jane face.

Church at Douala

At the church entrance, we were met by the Chaplain—a short, powerfully built man in a white cassock. Carl introduced him as the port captain, and when he came to know I was from the ship in town, he displayed even white teeth, as he was the man who piloted the vessel the previous night during the shifting. When he commented that he had not seen me, I had to explain to him that, being an engineer, I was deep inside the ship during manoeuvres. A few words of welcome were mentioned.

The previous service was going on. I could see on the board that there are 4 services on Sunday—in French, English, the local African language, and again in French.

Carl told me that the Pope had ordained some 15 churches in Africa and this is the one that does it for Cameroon. I look around and the church has a spacious compound (about 4 grounds) for car parking. Along the edge abutting the main road was a string of shops selling Christian trivia. There were a few mango trees, almost overflowing with raw mangoes.

The previous service was over and the crowd spilled out. I tried to observe the people, but the only thing that struck me was the riot of colours. Some of the ladies are wearing the traditional dress and a hat. The hats were more like a turban with peaks. Very few men sported a tie, and most of them were in plain t-shirts or colourful tops.

We entered the church and seated ourselves up front on the right side. The time was 0810 hrs. The seats were hard, wooden pews, and there was a wooden kneeling bar as well. No comfort or luxury here! The ceiling was high and lined with wooden arched windows along the sides. As we entered, we saw a dark wooden crucifix on the right, about 10 feet high. There was a white chain-link fence around, and many flowers were thrown inside. Perhaps a place for dedication! Above the altar was again a huge crucifix. The altar itself was lined with Mother of Pearl.

Long stained glass windows surrounded the Vestry, which had about 10 chairs around the periphery and a long table across. The place was decorated with some strange flowers with multicoloured leaves. At the head of each side vestibule was a small altar for Mass. The one on the right had a statue of Joseph standing with the infant Jesus. There was a podium ahead of us. The side walls had frescoes mainly about Christ and with a green-coloured base.

About 10 women and 5 men made up the choir, which was seated to the left. I believed this was a Catholic church, but I could see no confessional boxes. There were no fans, and the atmosphere was warm and humid. Not too bad, perhaps, because of the high ceiling.

The choir burst into song and the service was underway. There was no music to accompany them and also they were not following any notes. They sang by rote, and it was wonderful to listen to them. There were 2 Bible passages for reading, and both the readers went up to the mic together, while one waited for the other to finish. It was in English, but the accent was heavy and difficult to follow.

The sermon started off with a "welcome to our seafaring friends and thanks to Pastor Carl for steering us to church." The sermon was short and sweet.

Saying "yes" to God does not mean for one day only but forever. Similarly, saying "No" to God does not mean for one day only but forever. A good point, well brought up!

During the sermon, another priest walked around the congregation, waking up those who were falling asleep. For the offertory, 2 baskets are placed at the top of the centre aisle, and people go up and pay tithe. Carl and the German girl go up and pay; the 3 of us sit tight. There was no hullabaloo. The baskets were removed, and that is it.

The creed was read out by the priest. Participation by the congregation was minimal and reduced to sitting down and standing up. No prayer or hymn books are provided.

For communion, there is no kneeling at the altar required. People file past and receive only Holy bread; wine was absent. Some incense was burnt around the centre table and the service is over.

We piled into the van, and Sabine suggested going to the Mission for a soft drink. All of us agreed, so off to the club we went.

THE SEAMENS CLUB

The Seamen's Club at Douala was run by a German missionary group. When I first came here, I was quite friendly with one Wolfe who ran the show. Wolfe would have had problems handling the casual sex workers who plagued the place. He finally arranged it such that the girls were permitted into the club provided they were invited by one of the guests. Things ran well, but it kept out the decent crowd, and a reputation was established.

Wolfe was a short, slightly built German, and I suspect he put on a tough exterior but had a heart of gold. He wore his hair long (mid-shoulder length), and though cheerful, one could see he was under pressure. I never got to know him too well because the next time I came, he was gone.

During this time, the club had a TV and a pool table, a small library for magazines, and a bar. On the other wing of the 'L' shaped ground floor were the pastor's quarters and the office cum reception.

The rooms for a stay were on the first floor. In between was a swimming pool and a lawn with tables and chairs placed around for patrons of the bar.

When I next visited the club, Wolfe had been transferred to Lagos, Nigeria and a German couple had taken his place.

Between the 2 of them, they had managed to put a stop to the practice of sex workers visiting the place. One could see a more decent crowd using the facilities now. On Wednesday evenings, a group of American families, totalling about 25 people, regularly visited the place. A free helping of baked potato was served along with the brioche on Wednesdays, and I think it was this first steady income that turned the club around. Over the past 2 years or so, I was amazed at the change this couple had brought about in the club. The library had grown from a few German magazines to about 500 books and novels in different languages. A VCR has been acquired, and the television has been hooked on

Seaman's Mission

to Cable TV. There was a Video Cassette library of some 100 videos. A two-piece band played in the evenings. An outdoor grille served brioche, sausages, and I don't know what else.

The area in front had been cleared of all shrubbery, and the ground was being prepared to accommodate volleyball, basketball, badminton, and mini-soccer.

Carl was of a slight build and about 5'7" tall. He had a crew cut (short hair) and wore glasses. In his mid-thirties, he was quite a friendly person, but he has sometimes shown flashes of toughness that surprised me.

If Carl handled the external agencies, credit for the efficient administration and management of the club must go to his wonderful wife, Elke. I found that she loved chocolates—milk white chocolates, without nuts, which she complained got between her teeth. She was delighted to get German chocolates from Hamburg.

At the club after church, Elke served us coconut biscuits and chocolates. Soft drinks were offered, and the German girl had guava juice. Rick had coffee, and Elke and I opted for pineapple juice. The guava juice was bottled by a local lady and available only in Douala. It bore no labels. The pineapple juice was bottled by people known to Carl, so they could monitor the product and have it specially bottled to their taste.

During an earlier visit in June, I met Schmidt and Kathe, friends of Carl from his University days. We had been to a fancy restaurant for dinner after which Elke invited me into their home for the first time. There, I saw a great painting of the Crucifixion by a local artist. Green was the basic colour, but if you looked at it closely, you could see figures and other details. I believe they paid £300.00 for it. I loved it and asked if they could get one for me. I was told that the artist was usually drunk and that he would only make rare appearances at the club and that it was difficult to get him to paint. On this visit, they had a painting for me. Apparently, a group of German tourists had also shown interest, so they went up into the mountains in search of the artist. I believe he was a black fellow who wore his hair in long ringlets and lived in a house all painted in vivid colours. He enjoyed his hashish and drinks on which he binges regularly.

The painting they got for me was the same crucifixion scene, but the dominant colours were red and yellow. Carl clicked a picture of the 4 of us with his digital camera. Unfortunately, he couldn't give me a copy as he didn't have a printer, but he promised to email it to me at home and to the ship. The

4 of us were seated with the painting in the centre, and I was keen for this photo to get home because I wanted to know my wife's reaction to this!

Carl and Elke declined my invitation to Sunday lunch on board as they had to go to some sports park with friends. Elke was kind enough to invite me, but I declined. I was in no mood for sporting activity at this age!

Chinese Buffet on Sundays was gaining popularity. It was first mentioned by Ulf*, a colleague of Carl, and then by the second engineer on board. So, I decided to try it myself. A group of 6 officers from the ship planned to go. The second engineer arranged transport to pick us up from the ship at 1830 hrs. At about 1730 hrs, a pulley block from the baby boom of Crane 1 (port) started making noise, so the entire deck department opted out. That left only the second engineer and me going for a Chinese Buffet.

Abdul picked us up in his car at 1830 hrs, and we first went to a money changer where we changed US $50.00 at 650 CIFA to a dollar. Two places were having this Chinese Buffet—*The Oriental Palace* where the spread is smaller and the *Ristorante Chino* which is more expensive but better. We went to the Ristorante Chino, of course!

Port Warehouses from My Cabin

K.K. Ramagopal was our electrical officer and our raconteur or storyteller. He had a few yarns to spin every time we assembled for an evening drink.

THE CON ARTIST: Part 1 - The Lady

A newly married couple had gone to a cinema theatre to watch a movie. As customary, the bride was dressed up in a pattu saree and adorned with gold jewels. As they were waiting in the queue to buy tickets, a smartly dressed, good-looking girl approached the husband and requested him to buy a ticket for her. She was supposed to have been waiting till the last minute for her friend who had apparently stood her up. The gallant young man agreed, and the booking clerk issued 3 tickets together. The girl thanked them and after paying for her ticket, departed. Inside the theatre, after the husband and wife were seated, the girl reappeared and took her seat next to the wife. The movie started, and everyone watched with interest.

When the interval was announced, the girl leaned over and requested the wife to accompany her to the toilet as she was afraid to go alone. The wife conveyed the request to the husband who, gallant as usual, told his wife to accompany the girl. In the toilet, the girl knocked the wife out with some chloroform over the nose and disappeared with all the poor lady's jewels. After a long while, the husband realised his wife had not returned and went in search of her. He was aghast to find her unconscious in the ladies' toilet.

THE CON ARTIST: Part 2 - The Friend

A certain young man was employed by a company in the heart of Bombay city. Every day, he would take his scooter and drive down from his home in the suburbs to the nearest railway station, where he would park and take the train into the city.

One day, he found himself seated next to a boy a few years older than him, who struck up a conversation. Soon they were meeting regularly, and the young man divulged his home address, his family members, and the fact that he was driving a scooter without a licence.

One day, when there were only lady folk in the house, a strange man appeared claiming to be a close friend of the son. He was a charming speaker and had enough information to prove that he was indeed a close friend. He then said that the young man had been arrested by the police for driving without a licence and he urgently needed to pay Rs. 500 to release him and the scooter.

The poor lady parted with the money and the young man left to supposedly get her son out of jail!

Later, when the son returned home, he had to listen to a few choice abuses for driving without a licence. The reality, of course, dawned.

From Douala, we go to Tema (Ghana) and Abidjan before sailing to northern Europe. The sea condition from Gibraltar upwards was bad, with a swell of 4 to 5 metres. We are on the northern leg going from Africa to Europe.

On the Southern leg from Europe to Africa, we returned to Douala during the early morning hours of 21st February, Monday. We had loaded a parcel of 1000 tons of bagged wheat flour at Marseille to be discharged at Douala.

Discharge was going on with just the second officer Kumar* and 3 deck crew on night watch. At around 0200 hrs, when the tide was low, around 30 people swarmed onto the ship from over the side and the gangway. They went into the

Hold and started taking out bags of wheat flour. The crew had been advised not to interfere in such instances, and a diplomatic distance was maintained. One of the raiders noticed a Paint Store printed across a locked watertight door. He found the Duty Officer near #3 Hatch and collared him, holding a knife to his neck, as in the movies. The officer was pushed/dragged to the Paint Store at the break of the accommodation. They searched him for the keys to the Paint Store but found his cabin key instead. The raider tried out the wrong key, and when he saw it did not fit, started cursing and showing signs of violence. At this time, a police patrol passed on the pier, and the raider flung the key away and vanished. The Captain and Chief Officer were immediately aroused, and they found the poor Duty Officer a weeping, trembling mass. Cargo work was stopped, and port officials and police were called. They all arrived in about 10 minutes, by which time all the raiders had disappeared after loading 4 trucks full of goods. The final count was 19 tons of wheat flour short.

After sunrise on the same morning, Cadet Unni* went onto the pier to check the draft when an African came up behind him, held a knife to his neck, and asked, "What can you do if I cut you now?" Perhaps this was done only to emphasise that we were at their mercy. Unni threw up his arms in surrender.

The Captain called up the agent and told him he would be forced to depart (sail) if his crew were further threatened. As a precautionary measure, he cancelled all shore leave. I was disappointed as it meant no going to the Seaman's Club.

Evening visits to the club have been pleasant for me. During Wolfe's time, I had experienced mosquitoes there, and repellent coils would be provided by the club if requested. The menace has not been too bad on subsequent visits, perhaps because it is seasonal.

Carl and Elke were to circulate among the guests, but while Carl continued, Elke would stay put with me, and we both really enjoyed our conversations. One particular table in the corner, which had a thatched roof, was called the *Stammtisch*, Elke explained. Stammtisch literally means tree stump. In villages in Germany, the regulars at the local bar or the old-timers at the village square had a special place which was, by unwritten law, reserved for them to sit around. In the village square, this was sometimes a tree stump, hence the term Stammtisch.

Elke and Carl met at a disco. At that time, Carl was into youth counselling along with a friend, Schmidt, who was to later visit him at Douala. Carl's visiting card says he is a pastor, but I doubt it. Perhaps he just agreed to take up this job. In his house, he had email, a satellite phone, and so on. Every day he sent a report of all the ships in port and the ones he had boarded/visited to his office in Germany. I suspect his job was more information gathering for commercial reasons.

About 3 of the Germans I met at the Mission were introduced as Brewmasters. It appeared the Germans had set up a few beer factories here, and the locals really loved their beer. All the Malt and Hops were imported from Europe. One white guy was pointed out to me as the local Butcher. He was there because he knew how to cut the beef the way the whites wanted it.

Every evening, the club has 2 musicians. They sang old songs and played a crude-looking instrument, which was basically a xylophone made with the shells of some sort of vegetable acting as resonance chambers. They were not paid, but after a one-hour session, they went around collecting tips.

The French had issued 2 currencies in Africa—the CIFA (central) and the CIFA (west). Cameroon uses the Central CIFA. From 500 CIFA, the exchange rate is now 650 CIFA (central) to the US dollar.

Loading 'sinkers' by Barge

A beer at the club costs 800 CIFA, so a 100 CIFA tip to the musicians is considered handsome enough.

We loaded logs (timber) in Africa. Huge trees were cut in the mountainside forests, trimmed into logs, and sent down to the harbour. There were different varieties of wood. Some of them had a low density and floated on water. These were called 'Floaters' and were just pushed into the river, finding their way down to the harbour. Certain woods like (Ebony and Teak) are heavy. They were called 'Sinkers' and had to be manually brought down from the hills and then loaded onto the ship.

The Captain, Gurmeet, and I took Carl and Elke out for lunch. We went to a place called *La Fourchette*. It had a small pebbled parking area in front;

the inside was spacious and tastefully decorated. The bill read Restaurant - Bar - Pizzeria - Salle de Squash, so I imagined there was a squash court inside somewhere. We met the French husband, who was the owner. I believe the wife was German.

On the walls were beautiful paintings, all displayed by the artist concerned and offered for sale. Excellent work!

The food was excellent, and the price was quite reasonable. The total came to CFA 32,900 (a fixed menu was offered at 5,500 each), which worked out to $47.00 or Rs. 2000.00.

Some of the prices we paid:
$ &
Green Salad 1.43/62.00
Grilled Beef Fillet 6.86/300.00
Beef Fillet Roquefort 8.29/360.00
Half Pitcher of Red Wine 6.43/280.00

The same evening, Elke invited the Captain and me to join some of her friends for dinner. We went to a restaurant called *Les Beaujolais*. Again, tastefully decorated with paintings on display. We were a motley crowd, and we sat at a big round table. The guest list included:

1. Ms. Mary, Head of the English Language and teaching English at the British Council
2. Lady pilot with DHL
3. South African gentleman, also a pilot with DHL
4. Elke
5. British gentleman who was into timber export
6. German Beer Master whom I met at the club
7. German Beer Master's African girlfriend
8. Captain
9. Lady pilot with DHL
10. Self

The evening was full of laughs, and I really enjoyed myself. I again had a beefsteak, which came to 6000 CFA, but it was not as good as the one at La Fourchette.

SAN PEDRO

San Pedro is another port in the Ivory Coast, so a curfew applied. With the militia roaming the streets, no one was keen to get caught ashore in the evenings.

Mr. Kabon was the boss of the local stevedoring agency. He was developing his own rubber plantation on the outskirts of San Pedro and invited the Captain and me to see it. So on a bright, sunny afternoon, we took off in his car.

San Pedro was a much bigger town than I had earlier imagined! The road running parallel to the seaside was quite long, and there were marketplaces, a bus terminus, and so on. San Pedro looked deceptively small because most buildings were dilapidated, single-storey affairs. Not many buildings had more than 2 floors. I am talking about the Main Road only because there were some splendid private residential bungalows.

We drove straight along the main road. Abidjan was about 350 kilometres by road, but that road was out, so we took another route that was 500 kilometres long but a much better road.

San Pedro Main Road

After about 5 kilometres, we came to the edge of the city and across a roadblock. Big tyres and empty oil drums painted red and white form the barricade, and it is manned by about 10 soldiers. Military, paramilitary, police—all seemed to wear the same army camouflage colours in Africa.

A broad fellow approached our car. He was dressed in a dirty army uniform with a light blue beret, and sunglasses, and carried a machine gun. I was a bit nervous, not because of his size but because his machine gun may go off. Mr. Kabon seems to be well-known and after a look in the trunk of the car, we were waved through.

After the checkpoint, the road is superb! A beautifully topped, two-lane affair, but there was only the road—no lights, no signs, no nothing! On both sides were small hillocks covered with thick, green jungle. The road was undulated and winded. Sudden open patches appeared along the way where cows grazed and a river flowed swiftly through.

I believe some years ago the Chinese tried to introduce rice cultivation here, but Africans were not good farmers, and the project fizzled out.

After about 10 kilometres, we turned into a dirt road. The plantation occupied 3 hills and covered 35 acres. Mr. Kablon paid 1.5 million CFA ($2,300.00) per acre. He had 5 labourers working and he paid them 10,000 CFA per month. He also built living quarters for them and let them grow corn.

The rubber trees were 6 months to 2 years old. The yield was expected after 6 years of growth. The trees had to be sprayed with a pesticide to kill weeds once a year. The rest of the time the labour was only busy clearing away wild growth.

We visited their quarters and I was struck by their simplicity. Three structures were laid out in a square with a small square-shaped well in the middle.

The structures had tin roofs with mud walls cemented over. Building the mud walls was a special skill, and they had people from Benin coming over to do it. The quarters had crude doors but no windows and no sign of electricity.

There were many papaya and banana trees around and many, many chameleons. A shaggy ram goat with a vicious pair of horns was tied up to a tree, perhaps to provide meat someday.

Behind the structure were 2 elevated platforms, each about 2 square metres, on which ears of corn were stacked. A wood fire was built underneath to smoke-dry the corn. After all the ears were ripe, the kernel was ground to a powder to make a variety of dishes. Mostly gruel, I suspect.

We were greeted by a young woman dressed in a black sleeveless vest and knee-length wrap-around, speaking French. Her hair was tied in many small plaits, and she had a pleasant face with white, even teeth. There was a two-year-old chubby boy who I think was her son.

Of the 2 men who were present, one was a tall, middle-aged fellow with curly greying hair and a sparse moustache and beard. His teeth were brown, and his weather-beaten face was deeply etched with tribal marks. When a boy reached adolescence, deep marks were cut on his face with a knife or spear to indicate which tribe he belonged to, leaving his face scarred for life. The man was dressed in a faded, light blue t-shirt and a tattered dirty sarong. Mr. Kabon told us that he was the owner of 5 acres of a cocoa estate, and shared it with his 2 brothers, so there was not enough money in it for him.

The other man was short and of slim build. There was hardly any hair on his head, and he gazed at me with his cheerful face. He was wearing a red t-shirt and faded jeans that were frayed at the knees. All of them greeted us in French and spoke with a lot of respect.

Language was a problem in Africa—each tribe had its own language, and none of them had a script. All of them were only spoken languages. Mr. Kabon himself spoke 8 languages and yet he was not able to understand the farmhands when they spoke among themselves. Only the ones who drift into the city learn to speak French.

We returned to the ship, and I was feeling well-informed, but there is very little written about Africa, and there is a lot that is yet to be discovered about this vast continent.

Meme* the Pilot

Meme, our pilot, was entering San Pedro. He invited the captain and me to dinner the next evening.

At about 1730 hrs, he arrived on the ship to take us out, so we quickly dressed and left the ship. Meme had an Audi, and he apologised for the air conditioning not working. We passed the restaurant where he ordered dinner, and then we drove up to his house.

View of San Pedro Harbour and our ship from Meme's House

Meme had a lovely house located on top of a hill that overlooked the harbour and our ship.

We sat outside under a mango tree and enjoyed the view. Meme offered scotch, beer, coke, and orange juice and interesting snacks like fried bananas, peanuts, biscuits, and a sort of roasted coconut cut into thin slivers. We asked Meme to tell us how it was made, but he said it was a lengthy and bothersome process. Meme's wife came to greet us, but unfortunately, she spoke only French. A tall, well-built lady, she has a quiet dignity. She ran her own dental clinic in town. Meme had 3 daughters and 2 sons. He planned to send his first daughter to Europe for graduation. The family priest, who can string together 2 words of English, joined us. He hinted he would like to visit the ship, but the Captain played dumb. The priest departed. Around 1930 hrs, the 3 of us left for dinner.

The restaurant was part of the town square. We were greeted by a fat, middle-aged woman who said she was Bernadine. She had large, floppy breasts and wore a loose white shirt and tight green pants. Meme was very friendly but insisted she was like his sister. Perhaps. She was from Liberia and spoke fairly good English. I believe she came here 13 years ago as a young girl and married a local. Now the guy had taken 2 more wives, and she was miserable and wanted to go back to Liberia.

The restaurant was a square room with 4 tables, chairs, and a bar. The porch, with a tin roof and enclosed by a wooden picket fence painted red and white, seemed to be a better bet. There was outdoor seating as well, but it was drizzling and we did not want to take a chance.

We were a bit early, but within a few minutes, the service started. Glass dinner plates, paper napkins, knives, and forks were being placed on the table. We were presented with 2 big plastic bowls—one with soapy water to wash our hands and the other with fresh water to rinse them.

The dinner arrived. On special request, they served cassava. Cassava is a root, like Tapioca, shredded to look like grains of rice and then steamed. It is rich in protein and very filling. Africans eat it in huge quantities but I can't put away more than 3 or 4 tablespoons. There are fried potato chips and we have chicken. Pieces of chicken have been marinated in chicken soup cubes with salt and 10 grilled slowly over a charcoal fire. The chicken pieces were served in a dish covered with chopped onion, tomato, and cucumber. Really tasty! We had fish, similarly prepared. A big fish, about 12 inches long, was degutted and grilled whole. Bernadine told us it is snapper but I believe Perch is more common.

As we ate, it started to rain heavily, beating down on the tin roof. There were some leaks, but we were in a safe zone. Bernadine opened a beer and joined us as we ate. I found the food delicious, but the atmosphere left much to be desired—hard tables and chairs with cheap plastic tablecloths, rain, thunder, and lightning, and a strange black woman making conversation. Captain later admitted he did not like it, but I enjoyed the food and had a good time.

If I am going to include the people I meet in my writings, then I must go back a few years so that I can include a girl called Elizabeth.

It took 10 hours of steaming from Abidjan to San Pedro. I was told the roads were very good and one could make it in 3.5 to 4 hours, depending on the traffic. San Pedro was a small town and the port was also quite small, having just 2 conventional berths and a RO/RO berth. The gate was a few minutes' walk from the ship and another few minutes over a small hillock brought us back to the sea coast.

The Captain took about 7 of us for dinner to La Langusta on the seacoast. As soon as we were out of the gate, we were surrounded by a group of about 10 girls, trying to get friendly with us. They were obviously sex workers, but how they hoped to get a customer from our group was beyond me. So what did they want?

The Captain and I managed to avoid them by briskly walking ahead, and as it was a short walk, we quickly reached the safety of the restaurant. The girls were, of course, not permitted inside, so we had a pleasant and undisturbed meal.

Langusta is Italian for lobster. It is readily available in this part of the world, and Europeans love it because it is a rare delicacy for them.

In San Pedro, La Langusta is a restaurant I enjoy going to. A large octagon-shaped hut forms the main hall with an entrance on one side and a bar on the left as you enter. You should occupy a table close to the beach, and you can hear the boom of the surf and the rustle of the wind in the coconut trees. Tables and chairs were strategically placed so that you were not in the path of falling coconuts.

The place was owned and run by a Frenchman called H* and his pretty wife V*. She was Spanish, not from the mainland but from the Canary Islands. They had a caged chimpanzee. Steamed prawns were served in the main course and we all dug in.

About 2 hours later, when we came out of the restaurant, the girls were still waiting for us outside. This time a girl latched onto me, and when I tried to shoo her away, she said, "What's wrong in just talking to me? I am a human being!" I felt ashamed, so I said to her, "We can talk, but you will only be wasting your time."

So we walked and talked. She was young, in her early 20s, and her name was Lisa*. She had to run away from Nigeria due to the political problems there and she was just floating around here—a nobody in a nowhere world. By this time, we were approaching the gate and I turned to look at her for the first time, waiting for her move, but she continued looking straight ahead. Pride! She wanted to ask for money but was too proud to beg for it. At the gate, I slipped a $5.00 into her hand. She flung her skinny hands around my neck, and I felt her press into me as she gave me a warm hug. When she withdrew, her eyes were moist with tears. I admired her spirit, and I am glad I did what I did. I never did see Lisa again, but she has found a place in this book.

POINTE-NOIRE - THE PEOPLES REPUBLIC OF THE CONGO

The Republic of Congo lies between the Republic of Gabon to the west and the Republic of Zaire to the east. The River Congo and its tributary Rivière Oubangui form most of the eastern boundary. On the northeastern side, it adjoins the Central African Republic and to the northwest, the Republic of Cameroon.

Congo has a short Atlantic coastline, about 129 kilometres in length, extending southeast to the mouth of the Rivière Massabi. The principal port is Pointe-Noire.

Formerly the French colony of Middle Congo, the republic became a member state of the French Community on 28 November 1958 and was proclaimed fully independent on 15 August 1960. The area of Congo is 346,000 square kilometres and has a population of 106 million. The capital city is Brazzaville, formerly the capital of French Equatorial Africa and situated on the north bank of the River Congo, at the southwest end of Pool Malebo (Stanley Pool). It is a busy riverport.

Most of the northeastern part of the country is covered with dense forest, and there is heavy annual rainfall. Rivière Sangha, one of the main tributaries of the River Congo, runs through the northeast part of the country. The inhabitants are mostly of Bantu stock, and the citizens are called Congolese.

The unit of currency is the Franc CFA (Central). Malaria is prevalent. Dysentery and other stomach troubles can occur.

Dockside: Pointe-Noire

View of the Port

A railway connects Pointe-Noire and Brazzaville. The country *is* not well served by roads, but motor roads connect Pointe-Noire, Cabinda, Boma, and Brazzaville.

Pointe-Noire

Railway station post office at Pointe-Noire

There is a large modern airport in Brazzaville and an airfield in Pointe-Noire.

Pointe-Noire is the principal port of the Republic of Congo and has a population of 1.4 million.

There are numerous factories and sawmills at Pointe-Noire. Palm oil production is an important industry.

From	To	Total Distance	Steaming Time	Average Speed (knots)	Port Stay			Remarks	
					Days	Hours	Minutes		
Livorno	Genoa	71	3.9	18.2	1	20	18		
Genoa	Marseilles	219	12.2	17.95	1	14	18		
Marseilles	Sete	69	3.8	18.16	1	6	54		
Sete	Barcelona	162	9	18	0	17	48		
Barcelona	Valencia	155	8.6	18.02	1	8	42		
Valencia	Dakar	1962	111.7	17.56	0	9	0	At Anchorage	
					0	21	30	In Port	
Dakar	Abidjab	1192	65.7	18.14	1	8	54		
Abidjan	Cotonou	413	23.3	17.73	1	3	48	At Anchorage	
					1	7	0	In Port	
Cotonou	Luanda	1108	64.8	17.1	1	4	0	At Anchorage	
					2	0	18	In Port	
Luanda	Libreville	656	38.2	17.17	0	1	36	At Anchorage	
					0	22	30	In Port	
Libreville	Douala	211	13.2	16.1	1	23	0	At Anchorage	
					2	10	36	In Port	
Douala	Abidjan	840	49.3	17.04	1	19	48		
Abidjan	San Pedro	158	8.7	18.16	1	14	18		
San pedro	Valencia	2958	171	17.3	2	0	54		
Valencia	Livorno	533	30	17.77	1	22	54		
Livorno	Marseilles	245	14.5	16.9	3	21	42	at Layup	18 days 1 hour 00 minutes
Marseilles	Salerno	507	30.2	16.8	1	10	54	At Anchorage	
					0	14	0	In Port	
Salerno	Livrono	316	19	16.63					
Livrono	Genoa								
Genoa	Marseilles								

Voyage Log of M.V. Kwanza